The Music Products Industry
A Textbook for Music Business Students

The Music Products Industry
A Textbook for Music Business Students

Anderson Publishing
2016

The Music Products Industry: A Textbook for Music Business Students

Copyright © 2016 by Carl Anderson

First Printing: 2016

ISBN 978-1-365-07360

Anderson Publishing
1225 W. Wonderview Dr.
Dunlap, IL 61525

Dedication

Thank you to my parents for believing in my dream to become a musician, businessman, and educator. This book is a culmination of those three passions! - Carl

Contents

About the Author

Carl Anderson is a 30 year veteran of the music products industry. Working as the general manager and buyer for one of the larger music retailers in the country, he has seen many changes in the industry over the years. Additionally, Mr. Anderson has taught the Music Business program for Bradley University in Peoria, Illinois for nearly two decades. Bradley's program is the oldest in the country and has served as the model for many other schools. He is an active musician, playing trombone in many groups from classical to jazz to rock.

Acknowledgements

I would sincerely like to thank Jim and Ede Kidder of Kidder Music Service, Inc. for introducing me to the music products industry and taking me under their wing with their business when I graduated from college. Their guidance and mentoring in not only the music products industry, but in the whole realm of business retailing was the foundation for my success both in the business world and the academic environment.

I would also like to thank the late Craig Schertz for his enormous contributions to the piano industry. He will be sorely missed and I was blessed to be able to rely on his insight when he contributed to this book. Additionally, Trent Keeling was an incredible resource for the description of today's commercial audio industry.

I am thankful to Dr. David Vroman who gave me the chance so many years ago to teach in such a nurturing environment at Bradley University. I especially wish to thank Dr. Todd Kelly for challenging me to write this book. Without his encouragement this would have remained but a dream.

CarlAnderson

Forward:

The Greatest Show In The Land

There are some events in life that simply change your perspective. Such was the case when I stepped foot onto the trade show floor of my first NAMM Show. Inside was a musical circus with all kinds of crazy acts going on in every direction. There was a cacophony of sounds from thumping drums, ripping guitars, and blaring trumpets; like some kind of Charles Ives production. It was breathtaking.

I was a young trombone player from the Midwest, fresh out of college and knowing very little of the music industry. The local band instrument retailer in town was my only real connection to this world in my past, and now I was working for them. It was a short-term gig, just to get by until I found a "real" job. Twenty eight years later I found myself still there, now as their general manager, captivated by the excitement of the industry.

My boss had taken me to my first NAMM Show. I didn't really understand why I was going. I certainly did not have any buying authority in those days. Years later I would come to understand as I watch my students and young employees experience their first view of the "show". He wanted to see the expression on my face as I took my first look, and I have enjoyed seeing the next generation replicate that experience for themselves.

But, the craziness did not end there. My boss told me to quickly grab an instrument from anywhere on the trade show floor, throw them my badge so they knew who to blame if it didn't return, and assemble in a back room because the parade was about to start. Parade? Yep, the Fernand Petiot Jr. All Industry Marching Band. Or, as I would later know it, the "Bloody Mary Band". Petiot was the fabled inventor of the Bloody Mary drink and there were plenty of those being passed around backstage as we assembled. I had grabbed a trombone from the King Musical Instrument company and met up with my boss who had snagged a trumpet. Speaking of trumpets, one of the players in this rag tag parade band that was being created was none other than Doc Severinsen! My hero, who I had watched ring in Johnny Carson every night, was blowing trumpet right next to me!

But the next person who I would meet would really change my life. My boss introduced me to a gentleman holding a Vito clarinet and said, "I want you to meet Larry Linken. He is the executive director of NAMM. He puts this whole show together." Larry graciously welcomed me to the industry and said, "This is the greatest show in the land!"

And he was right. For a musician I had discovered the North Pole. It was real and it was in Anaheim, California. On top of that, I had just met Santa, whose elves in the halls of the trade show floor represented every possible musical product imagined.

The band quickly assembled for a one-time read through of "When the Saints Go Marching In" and we proceeded to stroll through the halls "officially opening" that year's NAMM Show. As we paraded down each aisle the vendors clapped and cheered us on as if we had just liberated a captive town in some distant land. The next four days were magical. I got to meet many of the leaders of the industry in some of the most casual settings. All of them wished me the best in the business and told me they would never trade the opportunity to work in the music products industry.

I have been to countless NAMM Shows since, but never was there one like my first. I was hooked. The show still opens with that crazy band parading around the halls. While the faces and companies and products have changed over the years, it is still The Greatest Show In The Land!

Carl Anderson

Introduction

Our Special Product

First a word from our Author...

Many industries have trade organizations that bring together many segments as a united front to assist the growth of the product or service they represent. Our industry in some ways is no different. But, in other ways I think our product is unique. Music is fun. Music is educational. Music is cultural. Music is life. But, is music necessary? This is a hotly debated subject when it comes to things like school budgets or public fine arts funding. But, few will contest that music is perhaps one of the most primordial attributes of humanity. *"Music is a moral law. It gives soul to the universe, wings to the mind, flight to the imagination, and charm and gaiety to life and to everything." Plato*

While few would dispute the words of the philosopher, Plato, the commerce of music does not just happen. In our society, music, like so many things, often reaches down to the lowest common denominator if not guarded by the champions of the art. So, while music has permeated every culture known to man since the dawn of existence, the definition of music has changed and morphed through the ages. More importantly, however, is how our current culture often treats the value of this art form. In the rushed culture of our modern society, music is both revered and challenged for a place at the table. When push comes to shove, we are dealing with a

1

product that may be culturally necessary, but takes a back seat to the agenda of both politicians and pundits alike. It is challenged both for funding in our educational system and our public culture. It is a constant struggle to keep the spirit of Plato in the minds of the next generation of music makers.

And, that is really the underlying task behind the myriad of trade organizations that pepper our industry. While culturally significant in the bigger picture, it competes daily for attention in a world with so many diversions. It is a product that one can live without, albeit with fundamental cultural bankruptcies. At the end of the day, music is viewed as a luxury by many and a diversion by most. We sell entertainment for the soul. And, while most of you reading this textbook are probably musicians and have a notably different perspective than much of our culture, we still struggle to keep our product as a fundamental necessity to mankind.

So, we must understand that our competition is all of the other diversions that are in the marketplace. Does a child start piano lessons or gymnastics? Band or soccer? Guitar or scouts? Even if music is added to a child's educational pallet, it is often compromised by a society that programs students' daily lives to the point where the passion of a music lesson becomes just another hurried activity between school, homework, and ball practice. Our true competition, then, is all of the other noise in our society grasping at both people's time and dollars.

Our music product, then, is different than many others industries. And, the music products industry is different yet. Unlike the recording industry, the music products industry services the actual musicians themselves. Whether they be beginning amateurs or seasoned professionals, these are the people who actually make the music. Listening to a recording is a passive activity. Unlike popping an ear bud to your smartphone, it takes time and work to actually successfully use our products, Of course, it is that time and work that makes the product rewarding. Does the consumer simply "consume" the music by listening, or are they transformed into budding musicians themselves and opened to the creativity within? It is an active product, not a passive one. But that creates one more additional obstacle for the industry...to share the passion of "making music" not just listening to it. It is a higher level of experience that once a consumer tastes, is often hooked. But, it takes effort to get them to take that first bite.

So, ultimately for our industry to work, we actually need to create music makers. It is not enough to rely on people to "discover" a love for making music. We need to be proactive in our approach. This is often known as embracing the "abundance principle". One of my favorite authors, Dr. Steven Covey, wrote an immensely influential book entitled "The Seven Habits of Highly Effective People". He spoke extensively about the concept of embracing an abundant principle approach to a market. That is, we must not assume the marketplace is limited. If we do, we will expel a great deal of energy simply trying to rob market share away from someone else; like trying to steal guitar sales from the store down the street. Rather, by focusing on the creation of new markets and new musicians, we increase the pie for all those at the table. This is not only a vastly more efficient and less expensive approach, but it benefits the over-reaching cause of music advocacy which drove so many of us to this industry in the first place.

So, we introduce the alphabet soup of trade organizations. While each has a segment of the industry dear to their hearts, they all share the same united passion and goal to increase and strengthen the industry by ultimately expanding the pool of music makers. Each has provided unique tools to help retailers and manufacturers alike promote that cause. So, let's get started.

The Music Products Industry

Chapter 1

The Alphabet Soup of Trade Organizations

NAMM

NAMM stands for the National Association of Music Merchants. In an effort to redefine its more global impact on the industry, the official name changed a few years ago to the International Music Products Association or IMPA. However, NAMM had become such a fixture in the vernacular of the industry, today the NAMM name has stuck. It is controlled by an elected board of directors, made up of retailer owners and supplier representatives. It hires a professional staff to administer the objectives of the organization.

NAMM represents the entire $17 billion dollar music products industry and acts as the umbrella organization for a plethora of other trade organizations that specialize in particular product segments. Founded in 1901 NAMM has grown immensely over the last century and hosts one of the largest trade shows of any kind on the planet. Its mission is simple: "Strengthen the music products industry and promote the pleasures and benefits of making music." Fundamentally, it creates music makers and connects them with the products they need. To achieve that end, NAMM focuses on several key activities.

First and foremost NAMM hosts trade shows. The grandaddy show of all shows is what is simply known in the trades as The NAMM Show. While all of their shows are NAMM shows, the annual show held in Anaheim, California each January is the king. This show covers over five football fields worth of products and is closed to the general public, except for an occasional consumer day. You must either be a retail dealer, manufacturer, endorsed artist, press, or special guest to attend. Even so, over 95,000 people find their way onto the show floor each year. The primary purpose of the show is to introduce new products to the retailers and to write business. To do this hundreds of exhibitors spend thousands of dollars creating elaborate booths to showcase their wares. Buyers are distinguished by their notable blue badges, that act as targets for vendors. An enormous amount of yearly sales are done in the four days of the show.

While the NAMM Show is certainly the biggest, NAMM puts on several other shows throughout the year. Each July, Summer NAMM is hosted at various Midwest venues. Most successfully has been the show in Nashville and a new convention center was built to help accommodate this show. While much smaller than its big brother in Anaheim, it provides accessibility for some dealers that are not always able to make the larger show. It also enables vendors another opportunity to promote orders for upcoming holiday sales. Each spring in Frankfurt, Germany NAMM hosts an international show for the European market. And, recently, the Musikmesse Show in Moscow, Russia has been established to reach this market. Most recently, there has an explosive growth in NAMM's newest show, Music China, which takes place in Shanghai. Other smaller shows around the globe work to make this trade organization live up to its new moniker as a truly international organization.

The second function of NAMM is to strengthen its membership base so that all people and organizations in the music products industry are on the same marketing page. Currently, there are more than 9000 industry members consisting of both retail owners and suppliers. This allows a synergy of effort when approaching common industry challenges. NAMM has lobbied for changes in laws and policies to promote fair trade for the industry. It works through strength in numbers and is always focused on increasing its membership base.

The third target for NAMM is that of professional development. Drawing on the collective success of its membership, it is the responsibility of NAMM to help educate its partners to be strong businesses. This is done through a variety of seminars, both online and at its shows. Most notably is "NAMM University" which hosts both hour long talks from industry leaders as well as smaller 20 minute mini-clinics throughout the trade show day from volunteer members who have expertise on certain techniques.

As part of its professional development, NAMM has reached out to Universities with music business programs to connect with the next generation of music merchants. This "Generation Next" is a morph from an earlier organization known as NAMBI, or NAMM Affiliated Music Business Institutes. The previous organization was loosely organized by the various affiliated colleges. Now controlled directly by the NAMM home office in Carlsbad, California the program aims at encouraging students to focus their music business studies on the products industry. One perk is allowing students of affiliated schools to attend the NAMM shows to experience the industry first hand and make connections for internships and later careers.

Another outreach program to the next generation is NAMM YP or NAMM Young Professionals. Previously known as the National Association of Young Music Merchants, this organization is for people under the age of 40 who have begun their career in the music products industry. The new moniker reflects the emphasis on being the next generation of professionals, rather than simply being young. The president of this organization has a seat on the actual board of directors of NAMM to keep the youth of the industry connected.

The Music Products Industry

A fourth objective for NAMM, and perhaps one of its most important, is that of market development. As discussed earlier, for the industry to survive it must grow the market and keep its mission at the forefront of our culture. To this end, NAMM has created a myriad of initiatives, some of which are handled in-house, and others are promoted by sub-organizations that are under the general NAMM umbrella.

One of the strongest initiatives has been to keep music education as a fundamental core curriculum in our schools. As most are aware, this often is one of the toughest fights as shrinking school budgets and demands for standardized testing often overshadows the importance of the arts. Whether testifying in front of a Congressional panel or speaking to a local school board, NAMM considers the importance of music education to be one of its highest priorities.

However, public schools are just one avenue for music making. An even more-sizable market is the general public and NAMM campaigns constantly about the sheer enjoyment that music making creates. While many often connect our industry with seasoned, professional musicians, the real market exists with "recreational music makers" who simply use music as an escape from the hectic realities of life. Much as a golfer takes to the links on a Saturday to enjoy the peacefulness of the environment and the camaraderie of friends, amateur musicians can pick up a guitar and transport to another world. Whether socially with others or playing privately in their living room, the amateur recreational music market is far larger than the professional one. And, of course, the road to professional starts with the first notes of a beginner. The directive of "Just Play" is NAMM's reinforcement that it matters not what the motivation, as long as you just join in the fun.

The final objective of NAMM's mission is to truly become a global partner. While initially a U.S. organization, NAMM has become an international player. A growing portion of the vendors at the trade shows are not U.S. companies and the distribution reach for musical products stretches to every country in the world. To reflect this, NAMM has expanded both its trade show presence as well as its advocacy programs globally.

The website for NAMM can be found at www.namm.org.

Music Achievement Council (MAC)
One of NAMM's affiliated organizations is the Music Achievement Council or MAC. Formed in 1983, this group acts as one of the main marketing groups to assist music educators with the recruitment and retention of children in instrumental school music programs. To this end, MAC has created a wealth of tools that teachers can use. There are tips for getting students interested in music or suggestions on how to create a school music budget. Its publication, "A Practical Guide for Recruitment and Retention" is practically the bible for young educators beginning a career in teaching music.

A number of years ago, Sandy Feldstein, former CEO of Carl Fischer Music composed a commissioned work for the MAC. Known simply as "First Performance", this band piece was designed to be played shortly after students had only learned 5 notes on their instrument. Since every student takes up an instrument with the concept of "performing", rather than simply "practicing", Mr. Feldstein recognized the importance of letting students perform "early and often" in their musical experience.

While the First Performance work could be performed independently with just beginners, two additional, more complex versions were also written for junior high and high school students, respectively. Cleverly designed, these three versions could be performed simultaneously, allowing the beginners to "sit in" on a real concert of more advanced students, giving them a taste of what was to come in future years.

The website for the Music Achievement Council can be found at www.nammfoundation.org/music-achievement-council.

SupportMusic.com

A similar support organization under the NAMM umbrella is SupportMusic.com. This website acts as a common portal for all research supporting the benefits of music making, specifically in our education systems. Hundreds of affiliates belong to this organization and contribute to its findings. For communities or schools suddenly faced with the prospect of losing a music program to budget cuts, this site has acted as a rescue vehicle to quickly gather the supporting research outlining not only the benefits of music, but its fiscal practicality.

Anyone concerned about music advocacy should join at www.supportmusic.com.

Mr. Holland's Opus Foundation

Inspired by the movie of the same name, the Mr. Holland's Opus Foundation was created as a portal for concerned individuals and businesses to donate money to fund the purchase and repair of musical instruments for school students. The movie's composer, Michael Kamen, started the foundation in 1996 to insure that all students have access to working instruments in their music programs. The foundation donates millions of dollars worth of instruments to struggling school systems that do not have the resources to make such purchases. Schools can apply for grants from the foundation. To qualify, at least 65% of the school's student population must qualify for the National Lunch Program. They also must have an existing instrumental music program that takes place during the school day as part of the regular school curricular activities. These grants are awarded in the form of new or refurbished instruments, rather than cash grants, to insure that the program's mission is respected.

You can visit the foundation's website at www.mhopus.org

VH1 Save the Music
A similar music advocacy program, known as VH1 Save the Music, was developed a number of years ago with a slightly different motive. While the Mr. Holland's Opus Foundation works to improve existing programs in financial need, VH1 Save the Music's mission is to establish new instrumental music programs in schools where they do not currently exist. In order to qualify, once again the schools must have a student population that is primarily under-privileged. Before receiving instruments and equipment through the grant, the school must commit and budget a full time music faculty member to teach instrumental music, and they must also commit to having the the music curriculum during the regular school day. Then, the foundation purchases instruments from a local music store to keep business in the school's local community. Once again, there are no cash grants as part of this program, only musical instruments and equipment.

You can visit the foundation's website at www.vh1savethemusic.org.

Guitar & Accessories Marketing Association (GAMA)
While many of the trade organizations we have discussed have a wider-reaching advocacy slant for the whole music industry, others work more closely with the retailers and manufacturers of the product segment they represent. The Guitar & Accessories Marketing Association or GAMA focuses on market development for guitars and related products. One of the more successful campaigns has been their Teaching Guitar Workshops, which educate music teachers in schools on ways to incorporate teaching guitar as part of their classroom curriculum. As part of this, they have also actively assisted in the funding of guitars for classroom use through corporate sponsorships.

Additionally, they sponsor and promote International Guitar Month each April as a way to target intense marketing interest in what is usually a relatively slow month in the music industry. Membership is limited to manufacturers and importers of guitars and accessories or publishers of guitar music.

You can visit the organization's website at www.discoverguitar.com

Percussion Marketing Council (PMC)

The Percussion Marketing Council or PMC is a relatively new organization, formed in 1995, and is the percussion industry's trade group. It's focus is to actively promote the art of drumming to people of all ages and to give a unified voice for percussion education. Like many of these advocacy organizations, the underlying goal is to expand the market and create new musicians to sustain both the art and the industry. Their "Percussion In The Schools" or PITS program has been successful in supplying professional drummers as educational facilitators for clinics in schools.

Unlike GAMA, PMC is open to both retailers and manufacturers of percussion equipment. PMC promotes the month of May as International Drum Month, which like the guitar industry, attempts to highly focus percussion awareness during this time of year. Retailers are encouraged to develop community programs and sales events during this month. Cooperative programs between the retailers and the manufacturers help to not only strengthen the market, but build industry alliances in the supply chain.

You can visit the council's website at www.playdrums.com

Percussive Arts Society (PAS)

While not directly under the NAMM umbrella, it would be remissive not to mention the importance of the Percussive Arts Society or PAS on the percussion products industry. This organization is focused on educating students and teachers on all things percussion. Its yearly Percussive Arts Society International Convention or PASIC is the largest percussion event in the world and brings together not only educators and percussionists, but the related manufacturers who display at this convention each November. Based out of Indianapolis, Indiana, the convention has now found a relatively permanent home there, but attendees come from all over the world.

You can visit the society's website at www.pas.org

National Association of Professional Band Instrument Repair Technicians (NAPBIRT)

Perhaps the longest acronym in the industry, NAPBIRT is the trade organization for technicians that repair musical band instruments. Born in 1976 by a group of technicians wishing to share tips on how to better facilitate repairs, this group has grown to over 1300 members from 20 nations. Educational seminars are held periodically at its training facility in Normal, Illinois and each year a national convention is held for its membership at various locations around the country. Additionally, the organization assists its membership to find employment opportunities at music stores and manufacturers.

You can visit the organization's website at www.napbirt.org

Retail Print Music Dealers Association (RPMDA)

The Retail Print Music Dealers Association was born in 1976; interestingly the same year as the most significant piece of copyright legislation was passed in the United States. The Copyright Act of 1976 re-wrote intellectual property rights as we know it today. The RPMDA was the creation of a handful of print music retailers that wished to address problems with the relationships between the retailers and the publisher of copyrighted music. Over the years this organization has strengthened that relationship and continues to be the voice for this part of the industry.

Both retailers and publishers are welcomed to join the organization and it has grown significantly over the last few decades in both size and influence. Each year a national convention is held, and both dealers and publisher get to spend a few days discussing the industry. Working sessions help the attendees to learn about changes in the industry, how to better manage their inventory, and how to cross market sheet music with other products. As the digital age continues to change how music is delivered, sheet music publishers and dealers alike have had to adjust their business models to stay relevant. RPMDA is a valuable resource for all of those who wish to make sure print music continues to be distributed profitably into the future.

You may visit the association's web site at www.printmusic.org

National Association of School Music Dealers (NASMD)
Created in 1962 by a group of music store owners that specialized in a new emerging music market in our public schools, the National Association of School Music Dealers has become one of the most important trade organizations in the industry. Today, its membership includes not only school music dealers but the major band instrument manufacturers that supply their product. While its function is to support this particular market, its real mission is to insure that children continue to make music in our schools. As such, its members are some of the loudest music advocates in our industry and work very closely with many of the aforementioned support organizations that sit under the general NAMM umbrella.

Each spring the NASMD holds a convention somewhere around the country and attracts hundreds of attendees who spend a week studying the industry and learning from each other. Keynote speakers from the industry address the membership, and breakout sessions and roundtable discussions allow for a week of sharing ways to keep the industry thriving. Many of its past board members have served on the greater NAMM board of directors.

Membership status is limited to a very strict set of requirements that insure its member dealers are indeed truly "school music dealers" and not just music stores that dabble in the product seasonally. These requirements exclude "online" stores, as its members must have a physical place of business open to the public. Members must have "road reps" that make sales calls to schools and must have repair facilities on site. Functionally, the dealers must have school music as a fundamental part of their business model and advocate for its continued support in our school systems. Its associate members are any manufacturers or suppliers that provide products to the school band market, and they help to underwrite the convention each year.

Please visit the association's web site at www.nasmd.com

In conclusion

While this is not a complete list of every music advocacy group or trade organization connected to the industry, it does reflect some of the most active and relevant in today's market. As you have seen, each provides its own twist to a particular favorite musical area. Regardless of their emphasis, all have an underlying mission to make sure music stays active and strong in our society. They encourage all of you to not only visit their websites or join their organizations, but to become part of a unified voice for music advocacy so that the arts continue to flourish for generations to come.

The Music Products Industry

Chapter 2

The Pro Audio Combo Market

The Marketplace

It was February 9th, 1964 and the music industry didn't know it, but the marketplace was just about to change forever. There are certain events in history that happen that have far reaching consequences, sometimes intended and sometimes not. No one in the music products industry could envision what was about to happen when four young, British teenage heart-throbs took the stage on the Ed Sullivan Show and broadcasted their new "Rock N Roll" music into the living rooms of homes across the country. Perhaps never in the history of the music industry has one event changed a marketplace so significantly.

The guitar, an instrument once relegated to folk music, had become electrified and so had an entire generation of kids wanting to learn to play it. The guitar had already started to become a popular instrument, due in part to Mel Bay's publication, "The Modern Guitar Method", which to this day is still one of the best selling beginning instructional books for this instrument. Equally important to its transformation was Les Paul, a guitarist-inventor who had experimented with creating a solid body guitar. His prototype guitar known as "The Log" is still on display in Nashville at the Country Music Hall of Fame Museum. His collaboration with Ted McCarty, then president of the Gibson Guitar Company, eventually produced the legendary "Les Paul" model electric guitar, which, incidentally is still featured on the cover of the Mel Bay Modern Guitar Method book.

The very first modern electric guitar can probably trace its roots to the Rickenbacker Company, whose iconic round body and long neck was made famous by the Beatles. However, it could be argued that it was Leo Fender, who had already created a successful solid body electric guitar, that would launch the music manufacturing world into the electronics age. Fender, a radio repairman turned inventor, would go on to create some of the most pivotal products for the music industry. His work perfecting vacuum tubes created the modern guitar amplifier. His Telecaster "Tele" guitar became the staple for the country music scene. His Precision Bass guitar or "P-Bass" will forever be the standard from jazz to fusion. But it was his Stratocaster model or "Strat" style guitar that is the single most-recognizable electric guitar style ever produced.

Over the years we would see other technical revolutions that would shape the industry. The vacuum tube would be later replaced by solid state electronics, making equipment lighter, cheaper, and more reliable. And, of course, digital technology would have a lasting impact, especially in the world of recording and audio engineering. Today, the pro audio combo market represents the largest market segment of the music industry and it is still dominated by the guitar and amplifier products.

There are several factors that have contributed to the guitar's iconic stature. While a difficult instrument to truly master, it is an easy instrument on which to begin. Its relatively low cost for an entry level model makes it accessible to almost anyone. It is a perfect instrument to accompany the voice of its player, and by learning just a handful of chords you have mastered a large percentage of modern pop music. The guitar can be used with nearly every style of music, from sacred to thrash metal. And finally, it is extremely portable to be used in almost every setting. Lets face it, few people whip out a trombone when sitting around a campfire. While all of these factors have contributed to its success, the fact that it is associated as standard equipment for so many pop music idols has made it the star it is. Young musicians aspiring to be the next Eddie Van Halen or Neil Young know that learning to play guitar will start them on that path.

However, the **Pro Audio Combo (PAC)** market consists of far more instruments than just the guitar. Banjos, mandolins, dobros, and a myriad of eclectic string instruments populate the market. The nearly meteoric rise of the ukulele in recent years has acted both as an entry product for aspiring future guitar players and as a solo instrument in its own right.

Also, included in this product category are the amplifiers that drive all of these fretted instruments. The vacuum tubes of yesterday were replaced by solid state semiconductor technology in more recent years. Much like the rebirth of vinyl for audiophiles preferring the warm sound of older technology, manufacturers have revisited the use of the vacuum tube on newer models. To do this, the signal is first processed through a vacuum tube at the pre-amp stage before proceeding through the solid state technology. In these cases both tube and digital technology has merged to create the best of both worlds. Some of today's modern amps use digital technology to mimic a variety of different models of amplifiers, allowing the musician to dial up whatever style he is seeking all from same piece of equipment.

Public Address, known simply as P.A. equipment, is the final category of gear that is usually included in the PAC market. This consists of power amps, speakers, monitors, mixers and effects units that work to amplifier instruments and voice. P.A. equipment in this category is meant to be portable in nature and should not be confused with the large Commercial Audio market that includes equipment for arenas or permanent installations for buildings. This will be discussed in a later chapter.

The Music Products Industry

Customer Demographics

The nearly limitless use of the guitar means that its customer base is almost as vast. From young children aspiring to be a future rock 'n roller to adults taking up an instrument for the first time, the guitar has acted as an easy way to jump into the world of making music.

Many musicians become extremely loyal to specific models and brands of instruments. It is not uncommon for a saxophone player to play on the same instrument his entire lifetime, limping it together as parts get worn. Often they complain that new instruments just don't have the "sound" of the vintage models. While perhaps true in some cases, this can also be due to the fact that wind instruments involve so much of the musician's body that a new instrument requires a significant learning curve to play in tune.
The guitar market is quite different. It is not uncommon for a guitar player to own many brands and models. They may switch out instruments as they play different styles to match the sound they are trying to produce. While certainly brand loyalty plays a part, most guitar players enjoy the nuances of many different instruments and tend to be more open to trying new things. Additionally, the relatively low cost of many models allows musicians to purchase new ones frequently. So, while the buying cycle of some musical products may literally involve decades between purchases, it may only take a few months before the guitarist gets that "itch" to see what the local music store has new.

Product Lines

The guitar market has two distinct product lines: acoustic and electric. The popularity of these two tends to ebb and flow dependent partly upon what is being played by the pop market stars. For years following the emergence of the rock and roll

20

era, the solid body electric guitar dominated the market. In more recent years, the acoustic market has seen a resurgence. Beginning students tend to start with acoustic instruments, due in part to simplicity and often lower cost, especially when factoring in the need for amplification. Of course, any guitar can be amplified with some type of pickup and acoustic guitars with built-in pickups have increased in popularity. These "acoustic-electrics", as they are known, retain the natural acoustic nature of the wood shell while allowing the musician to be amplified through a P.A. system.

Acoustic guitars come in a wide range of shapes and styles, but most fall into two basic categories: **classical** and **dreadnought** acoustic. Classical guitars are characterized by having nylon strings, a flatter and wider neck, and an open head stock. These generally do not have reinforcing metal truss rods built into the neck. As such, steel strings should not be used on these as the neck can easily warp or cause the bridge to pull away from the body. These guitars are meant to be plucked as much as strummed; used primarily for classical literature.

The more common body style is the "Dreadnought" body, first developed by the Martin Guitar Company. This style is characterized by an oversized body for greater acoustical resonance and a steel reinforced neck to handle the tension of steel strings. This has truly become the industry standard for most acoustic guitars. However, there are a litany of other body styles as well. Parlor guitars tend to have a smaller overall profile, ideal for younger players. Cutaway models feature one of the bouts indented to access the higher frets. Twelve string models double each string for greater volume and resonance.

One unique twist to the acoustic guitar body style was developed by Bill Kaman, an aerospace engineer specializing in building helicopters. Being an amateur guitar player, Kaman used a carbon-based composite to craft a parabolic bowl that offered greater amplification than the standard violin-shaped body construction. This "Ovation" brand guitar became the start of an entire music division of the Kaman Corporation that included percussion brands such as Gibraltar and Latin Percussion. Over time, this music division was spun off, creating KMC Music, which was purchased by the Fender Corporation. More recently, many of these proprietary brands were sold by Fender to Drum Workshop (DW Drums).

Today there are many twists to the basic acoustic guitar. Many types of woods and finishes are used to create a myriad of designs, many of which affect the timbre of the unique instrument. But the basics of the modern acoustic guitar has fundamentally changed very little over the years.

Electric guitars, on the other hand, produce their unique timbres through the guitar amplifier to which they are connected and any other effects products that might be connected. As such, a musician can significantly change how the guitar sounds simply by changing accessories. This fact helps to drive parts of the PAC market as well, because a new amplifier or effects pedal can produce what sounds like a completely different guitar.

An electric, solid-body guitar's main feature is its pickup, the little magnet coil placed under the strings that transfers the frequency of the vibrating string to the amplifier. Probably the most significant invention to transform the electric guitar into what it is today, was the creation of the "**Humbucker**" pickup. Previously, a single, electrified magnet pickup was placed under the strings. However, the single coil tended to be extremely noisy, picking up not only the string vibration, but other electronic "noise" and "hum" caused by power supplies, wiring, and just about anything else that these miniature antennas might perceive. To counteract this, two single coil pickups are placed side by side with opposite polarity. This double pickup literally "bucks the hum" and produces a clean, warm sound from just the string vibration. Many modern guitars feature both single coil and humbucker pickups with

22

switches that allow the musician to employ one or more of the pickups. While the humbucker produces the cleaner sound, the single coil is often used when trying to create a "dirty" sound often associated with harder rock music.

Today there are many, many brands of electric guitars. Probably the three largest players in the market, however, have been Fender, Gibson, and Ibanez. Fender and Gibson were American companies that had significant contributions to the invention of the modern electric guitar. The Ibanez brand is owned by the Hoshino company, a Japanese manufacturer that began by copying the styles of the popular American brands. Eventually, they were sued for infringement and later went on to produce their own unique styles. Ibanez saw some fairly explosive growth in the 1980s and picked up many endorsing artists. It remains today a fairly major player in the guitar market.

There are also many, many acoustic guitar manufacturers, but this product segment is also dominated by a few large players. Gibson, Martin, and Taylor have long been seen as making some of the finest acoustics. More recently, Japanese makers Takamine and Yamaha have taken some significant market share.

Most of the lower end models of guitars today are made off shore from the United States. The lower cost of labor and availability of materials has forced much of this. Higher end guitars still tend to be made in the U.S. which is still the largest market for PAC products.

The amplifier market was first created by the guitar manufacturers to power the products they were producing. Later, other manufacturers that specialized in amp technology exclusively began to dominate much of the market, especially for larger rigs. Marshall Amplification, a British company specializing in guitar amps, became the standard bearer in the industry. Its "stacked" approach used two speaker cabinets, one stacked upon the other, with a power amplifier sitting on top. Large shows often would use stacks and stacks of speakers across the back line of the stage, creating a literal "wall of sound" for the audience.

While the creation of the Humbucker pickup was designed to create as clean of a sound as possible with limited electronic interference, the modern rock guitar sound has often embraced such distortion. To this end, guitar amplifiers have "distortion options" to create fuzzy or "crunched" sounds when employed. To further this, distortion pedals and other effects processors are often connected to expand the wild timbres of the modern guitar amp sounds.

Much as Marshall lead the way in the guitar amp field, Ampeg did the same for bass guitar amplifiers. This iconic amp is still made in America. Originally produced by St. Louis Music, its president Gene Kornblum sold the company to LOUD Technologies in 2005. SLM was also the manufacturer for Crate Amps, another leader for many years in guitar amps.

The final component of the PAC category is that of P.A. equipment. Usually, P.A. gear is franchised in two ways. Commercial audio refers to the large permanent installations of sound reinforcement in commercial buildings and the giant rigs often associated with touring bands. The companies that handle this kind of product are not your standard retailer and will be discussed in a later chapter. Rather, P.A. equipment sold by PAC dealers refers to the more portable sound systems and basic recording equipment that are used by smaller bands and entertainers. These are designed to be relatively portable, although systems can become rather elaborate for larger groups.

Standard systems usually consist of a power amplifier, a set of speaker cabinets, monitor speakers, a mixing console, a set of mics, and cables to connect everything. Additional effects processors such as EQ units, compressors, and the like might also be added to the mix. Today, we see the use of more modern technology such as WiFi and wireless systems that have eliminated not only the cables on microphones, but the cabling between the mixing console and the power amplifiers. Mixing can often be done from the convenience of a tablet or even a cell phone; what was once unthinkable only a few years ago.

Sales and Marketing Strategies

There are two primary marketing strategies to drive sales in the PAC market. These are lesson programs and artist endorsements. Retailers rely on in-store instruction to increase the size of the market. Manufacturers, on the other hand, use artist endorsements to create brand loyalty for their products and recognition in the market.

Lessons

Lessons have long been a way for retailers to create new musicians. It is a proactive way to increase the overall pool of musicians by simply creating new customers. It adheres to the idea that the market is potentially limitless and from a retailer's point of view acts as the single best way to market the PAC products. Retailers not only gain income from charging for lessons, but each new student represents a new customer. As their skills increase, so does their demand for new instruments, accessories, and sheet music. Stores that focus on the educational side of the business keep customers coming into their stores on a weekly basis, even if they don't need to purchase anything. It simply drives repeat traffic that no amount of advertising dollars could support.

Lesson studios at music retailers are usually administered in one of two ways. The most common is to simply charge the independent teachers studio room rent. Teachers either are charged for specific blocks of time during which they can use the room, or are charged a fee per student that attends. The advantage of this system is that it keeps the teachers as independent contractors rather than employees. As such, the retailer is not responsible for the typical payroll taxes and personnel accounting issues that a regular employee would have. Generally, the teachers are charged with the responsibility of keeping track of their student's schedules and collecting weekly payments. The store simply invoices the teacher at the end of the month for the room rent. The primary disadvantage of this set-up is that the retailer has very little control of the lesson program. Often the retailer is at the mercy of the teacher's accounting to know how much to charge each month. Additionally, there are limits to how much "store loyalty" the teacher might have to the retailer. There is often nothing in place to police a teacher from suggesting a student shop at a different location or online retailer.

The other way to create a lesson program is to actually hire teachers as employees of the retail store. As employees, the teachers must adhere to the general policies of the store in the same way as regular salespeople would. Often, the store administers the lesson program completely, booking new students, scheduling lessons, and collecting lesson fees. Some instructors may also assist on the sales floor when not teaching, reinforcing the reason they are there...to sell stuff! Retailers will often charge students on a monthly basis, rather than a per-service basis. This can be collected up front at the beginning of the month, eliminating the problem of late payments from students. The retailer takes a percentage of the fees and the balance is paid to the teacher during a regular payroll period. The primary disadvantage of this program, however, is the additional cost of having more employees. The retailer must deduct payroll taxes and match FICA deductions. Some teachers may also see this as a disadvantage as there is little room to "hide" income. Lesson income is perhaps the most "under-reported" income as much is paid in cash and frequently outside of a retail setting.

As an additional incentive to in-store teachers, a retailer may offer a small commission on items purchased by their students. This encourages the teachers to suggest new materials, replace worn accessories, and upgrade gear. While a cost to the store, its benefits can be significant in additional sales. It also encourages the instructor to think of oneself as more than just a teacher, but a professional who is looking out for both the student and the store.

Endorsements

While lessons encourage the overall development of musicians and create a general demand for merchandise, artist endorsements direct that demand toward specific brands and models. Consequently, these are extremely important for manufacturers and many will go to extreme lengths to put their gear in the hands of today's superstar musicians.

Retailers visiting the NAMM show will often see these artists in the manufacturer's display booths endorsing the newest products. **Endorsement deals** vary widely in the industry. In some cases, artists are given merchandise by the manufacturers for free or at a very reduced cost. In exchange the artists are listed as official endorsing artists for their brand. Additional duties may also include guest appearances in booths, clinics in retail stores, photo shoots for magazine advertisements, and much more. Fees for such appearances can vary widely depending on the scope of the duties and the popularity of the artist. In many cases fees are restricted to only educational clinics or concerts, and the other activities are expected to be gratis in exchange for the discounted or free gear. Typically, major manufacturers have an artist relations liaison on staff to coordinate these activities and to recruit new artists to their roster.

Endorsement deals also often invite artists to be involved in design and development of new products. Often they have access to company atile production shops to try out new technologies or design changes. In some cases, more popular artists might be invited to participate in the design of signature models reflecting the special styles or needs of the artist.

Whether the artist has his or her own signature model or not, endorsement deals insist that the artist actually perform on the brands they endorse and be sure to acknowledge these sponsorships whenever they do clinics and other educational activities.

Other Marketing Strategies
The Pro Audio Combo market tends to be extremely seasonal and follows much of traditional retail. That being said, most retailers move much of their yearly product in the last two months of the year during the holiday shopping season. A smaller secondary sales season pops up in the spring as customers receive tax refunds and find the itch to get a new guitar too strong to resist. This is one of the reasons that GAMA has introduced April as "Guitar Month" with additional marketing support at an industry level. This also helps what is often a pretty soft time of year for almost all retailers.

Lessons are often bundled as part of combo sales to encourage new students and to make sure that what might have been a passing impulse buy has longer sustainability. In some cases, retailers will offer a free lesson or two with the purchase of an instrument to get the students "hooked" and become a customer for life.

Supplier-Dealer Chain

In most cases the relationship between the supplier and the retail dealer for Pro Audio Combo products involves some type of franchise **dealer agreement**. While some low-end imported products might be sold through a wholesaler, most manufacturers handle their own distribution systems. Generally speaking, the higher priced products have some of the most restrictive dealer agreements. These agreements are often quite territorial in nature. Manufacturers wish to have adequate representation in a given population source, but also allow the franchised dealers to make a profit. Creating too many dealers in the same territory dilutes the market, thins margins, and discourages dealers from investing in significant inventory.

As you might expect, dealer agreements vary widely depending on the manufacturer. Generally, well established brands can enforce stiffer terms as there is competing demand to represent their line. Less established brands may be more open to negotiation as they are trying to get a presence in the market. In any case, most dealer agreements at a minimum discuss inventory buy-in levels, territory restrictions, and pricing policies.

Inventory Levels
Often a dealer agreement requires an initial minimum buy-in **master order**. This master order may have the dealer purchase a minimum number of units and representation across all of their lines. For example, a guitar manufacturer may require the retailer to purchase student level, intermediate, and professional levels in perhaps both their acoustic and electric lines. Generally, the initial order must reach a particular dollar total as well. This is all done so that the retailer does indeed become a true representative of the franchise and not just cherry pick the manufacturer for a few hot items or to satisfy a special order.

Commonly, a master order is required each year to maintain the franchise and this may be tied to the previous year's purchases. So, the retailer may need to purchase a quota equal to last year's purchases plus a percentage increase. While there are often incentives tied to such an order, such as **extended dating** or **freight allowances**, it is easy for this to spiral out of control. If the brand is growing in the territory there is little problem. But as other brands are introduced to the store's mix or the marketplace shifts its allegiance to a competing brand, it may be difficult to afford this ever-increasing master order.

Territory Restrictions

A signed dealer agreement will often softly define a geographic territory to which the dealer has exclusive representation. In today's very mobile society and driven by non-traditional e-commerce methods, this has become nearly impossible to totally enforce. Dealer agreements will often contain extensive language about how or if their lines can be represented and sold through the internet, either through independent retailer websites or online commerce services such as Ebay and Amazon. In some cases, the retailer may be restricted to simply listing the dealer as an authorized franchisee, and prohibit online sales. Others may be much looser, especially manufacturers trying to get market penetration against larger competitors.

Regardless, most agreements restrict a franchisee from reselling their merchandise to a different unauthorized dealer. These **"sideways sales"** are prohibited unless to another franchised dealer and then these are usually facilitated directly through the manufacturer's district manager. Moving merchandise sideways has long been a way for retailers to balance their inventory with other dealers, especially when a particular model might be out of stock at the manufacturer.

Financing

Extended dating or other financing options from PAC manufacturers tends to be much more conservative than with other parts of the industry. This is due in part to the fact that there are so many more PAC retailers than other music retail segments and many of these are smaller, less experienced businesses. After all, who wouldn't want to start a guitar store? Unlike what we will see in segments such as the school or piano market, it is much easier to find combo manufacturers looking for market penetration. The nearly limitless number of PAC manufacturers means that it is relatively easy to enter this market segment. Inventory buy-ins on some of these brands can be quite small and so there is less scrutiny in picking retailers. However, this also means that the trust level between manufacturers and retailers is equally small. Most vendors will either insist on COD (Cash on Delivery) for products or, at most, 30 day terms.

While other market segments often see the advantage of more extended dating for repayment, smaller combo dealers must practice great cash management to make it through the long haul. Today's sales are financing tomorrow's purchases. There tends to be a much more Darwinian approach to the PAC market. Many small retailers will open up, but few will survive the intense competition that multiple, similar retailers create. Added to this is the cut-throat pressure exerted by big-box guitar retailers and online e-commerce sites. As the strong survive, they are able to negotiate more-favorable terms with manufacturers, especially when entering prime retail sales seasons, such as the holiday market.

Financing inventory in general can be tricky and is often the one thing that can get retailers into trouble. Customarily, banks are resistant to finance inventory, short of a line of credit tied to personal assets of the owner. The high failure rates of small businesses, especially small combo stores, can translate to extreme risk for a financier. No bank will want to be stuck trying to liquidate a room full of Stratocasters if a music store goes bankrupt. The product is too unique and specialized to ever sell at auction for even a 10th of its value. As such, banks will generally stick to financing real estate, structures, and more generalized fixtures, rather than inventory.

So, the retailer is forced to look to the one party that has the most skin in the game, the manufacturer. It is to their advantage to have representation in their franchised stores, but they, too, are not immune to the high failure rates of PAC locations. Thus, they tend to be quite conservative about extending dating terms until the retailer has proven its creditworthiness over the long haul. Eventually, the larger retailers establish financing, but history is littered with large stores failing and leaving the manufacturers holding a pile of debt. In some cases, these "**big box**" stores have come to be seen as "too big to fail" and vendors have let unpaid, financed inventory build up to unmanageable levels. When they finally do succumb to the inevitable they have catastrophic effects on their suppliers.

In any case, financing terms and conditions will vary widely and will often be dependent on the history of the company and the relationships that are built between the retailer and the vendor over time. As trust is earned and solid repayment terms are satisfied, more credit can be extended. Still, it will always be a more conservative approach than is seen in other segments we will study.

Pricing Structure

There is probably no product segment in the music industry that is more price sensitive than the Pro Audio Combo market. While this may not have been the case when the segment was in its infancy, the explosion in the market over the last 50 years has meant that competition has been extraordinarily cut-throat. We will see that other segments have a much higher "**cost of entry**" and tend to limit the number of realistic competitors in a given territory. The relatively low cost of entry for a guitar or combo dealer means that most towns have multiple music retailers, many handling exactly the same brands and products.

The PAC market also has the largest overall customer base. As such, there are many manufacturers and dealers after this growing market. Added to this enticement is the entry of the big box retailers and e-commerce sites. Other market segments tend to require a higher level of customer/retailer interaction to create demand. All of this tends to exacerbate predatory pricing, especially by the larger retailers. Too often, a local retailer will cry "foul" to the vendor when, after spending large amounts of capital and time, the final sale is picked off by a national chain. Manufacturers tend to walk a fine line here. They wish to maintain the large network of smaller dealers that build the brand over the years, one customer at a time. But, they also are enticed by the large orders that a big box or similar vendor can afford and that keep their facilities operating at capacity.

To combat this, many manufacturers have attempted to establish **Minimum Advertised Pricing** policies. These **MAP** prices, as they are known, establish a minimum price that can be advertised for a product, either in print or online. It does not specifically establish a minimum sales price, as that could be considered restraint of trade. But, it tends to set the "street price" of a product in the marketplace.

The justification by the manufacturers for such MAP prices has been to keep the value of their brands from slipping below its competitor's products while recognizing that no one is likely to pay the full **Manufacturer's Suggested Retail Price**. In fact, **MSRP** really is just a set price point from which discount structures can be established and negotiated with retailers for quantity purchasing, and is rarely considered a realistic price to consumers. Rather, the MAP price tends to replace MSRP as the real price marketed in the stores.

In reality, manufacturers create MAP pricing policies as a compromise between the small, independently-owned retailers and the larger big-box and e-commerce players. It attempts to prevent a "race to the bottom" in pricing competition. The vendors need to maintain a network of smaller dealers that penetrate all sizes of communities and maximize their sales nationwide with the representation that the larger stores can offer. MAP basically establishes the net margin a retailer will attain for a given product. The constant argument tends to focus around just where these MAP levels are to be set. Too low of a MAP price and the smaller retailer cannot adequately generate operating capital to maintain its business model. Too high of a MAP price and the big stores argue that they are losing the advantages of their economies of scale and the pricing pressure they can exert in a market in lieu of more extensive services.

To combat this ongoing battle, both large and small retailers often look to **proprietary brands** to get away from the restrictive pricing policies often regulated by established brands. If consumers can find the exact same product from multiple sources, they will often simply pick the retailer with the lowest price. This "commodity" pricing model, where the product itself is indistinguishable in the market, causes the "race to the bottom" we have discussed and destroys margins for all sizes of retailers.

Proprietary products are brand names or models that may be unfamiliar to the consumer. Their limited distribution may make it difficult to compare prices. In some cases, these can be specific models with a familiar brand name, but only marketed through either big boxes or small dealers. Either way, the opposite-sized retailer does not have access to this model and thus, they can build loyalty to this model at their specific stores. They can also obtain a better profit margin by establishing pricing unique to this product that cannot easily be found elsewhere in the market. Often these models do not even show up in the manufacturer's website.

Another form of proprietary product is to create "**house brands**" or "**stencil brands**". These are often products made by a familiar manufacturer but branded with the name of the retailer, buying group, or similar purchaser. Lacking the manufacturer's trademark, these do not dilute the established brands of the vendor, but allow for further manufacturer sales. Usually, these must be purchased in quantities adequate to justify the branding. Large retailers may be able to support this. Smaller ones often belong to retailer buying groups that share this brand, but allow distribution to be diverse enough to keep from competing with each other. Either way, the purpose is still to sell product and support margins by avoiding direct competition.

Future

The Pro Audio Combo market has a large product base. As such, some is much more subject to technological improvements than others. However, it has historically been a market segment with a fairly high **turn cycle**. That is, consumers tend to look for the newest and fanciest model to hit the market. Perhaps in this segment, more than any other explored, consumers look to constantly replace their gear in shorter **buying cycles**. This creates the large market that attracts so many start-ups. It is also the reason why this product segment represents so much of the floor space at the NAMM Show each year. It thrives on constant reinvention much more than other parts of the music business.

One of the challenges to this product segment has also been a limiter on other parts of the industry. Today's pop scene has focused very heavily on vocalists, many of which do not play an instrument. This has been especially the case with the electric guitar market. There is no "Beatles effect" driving the electric market. The acoustic guitar market has seen significant growth over the last decade, due in part to strong growth in the country music market, however.

Another challenge that this market segment has tackled is the development of female market. Led in part by the efforts of Tish Ciravolo, founder and president of Daisy Rock Guitars, there has been significant growth in the female guitar market, including electrics. Continuing to grow this untapped market will help future sales in the entire PAC market.

Manufacturers continue to expand their production to developing nations to control costs. This keeps margins higher for the manufacturer and prices lower for the entering consumer. As the market develops, brand loyalty can be established at the retail level with its established distribution network. With an eye for continuous market expansion by creating new musicians from a virtually limitless supply of eager youth, the PAC market will continue to thrive.

Chapter 3

The Percussion Market

The Marketplace

In the same way that the infamous appearance by The Beatles on the Ed Sullivan Show sparked a shock wave that would transform the guitar market, it would also ignite the percussion market. When Ringo Starr appeared behind his classic Black Oyster Ludwig drum set, America and the rest of the world wanted to become a rock 'n roller. The concept of the modern drum set had been around since shortly after the turn of the last century when William Ludwig, Sr. invented a workable drum pedal that allowed the bass drum to be played by a foot. From there other drums and hardware would be added and today's drum set began to take shape.

Almost as important to the percussion market's growth was Remo Belli's invention of a reliable synthetic drum head. No longer was the drum dependent on fickle and expensive calf's skin for its heads. Now drums heads could be made cheaply and in any size and shape imaginable. Remo is still the largest manufacturer of drum heads in the world and can be found on nearly every brand of drums.

But the percussion market is more than simply drums. It is truly the oldest music product segment in the industry. Virtually every culture around the world has included some sort of percussive instrument as part of the history of their ritual and song. Avedis I, a Turkish alchemist discovered a secret for treating alloys and invented the modern day cymbal in 1622. Using the name, Zildjian, or "son of cymbal maker", his family would go on to found the oldest continuing business in the world. To this day, Zildjian is still the flagship cymbal company for the music industry.

More recently we have seen an absolute explosion in the ethnic "world" percussion market. There is a seemingly endless array of both tuned and un-tuned instruments and hand percussion "toys" that contribute to this market. As the industry becomes truly global in nature, influences from virtually every culture have contributed to the current market.

Customer Demographics

Practically everyone at one time or another has wanted to be a drummer. Whether it was as a little child beating on your mother's pots and pans or a young teen visiting a music store, it is easy to get mesmerized by the sheer volume of percussion instruments. Contributing to this is the fact that anyone can make a sound on virtually any drum by just hitting it. There are no special buzzing lips or vibrating reeds involved. If you can smack it, you can make a sound! Of course, mastering the instruments is an entirely different story. And, unlike other families of instruments, a true "percussionist" can spend a lifetime learning how to play everything.

Even the percussionist's notation can be foreign to other musicians. While tuned instruments, such as the xylophone or the timpani use traditional notation in either treble or bass clef, un-pitched instruments such as snare drums, cymbals, or any of the hand percussion items, use a modified syntax. This somewhat "foreign" language of notation adds to the uniqueness of today's percussionist.

Customers tend to fall into two separate musical camps. Classical "percussionists" with more traditional training either in school or through private study tend to learn how to read music and play a wealth of instruments beyond basic drums. "Drummers" interested in playing pop music often will only learn how to play the drumset and many may never learn to read any type of notation. While perhaps scorned by true "percussionists", whose reading ability allows a much broader approach to the entire musical family, the basic "drummer" makes up the overwhelming majority of the market.

For many, playing drums is as much about recreational music making than conquering the fine art of orchestral percussion. In fact, one of the fastest-growing activities involving the market is the "drum circle". Led by a facilitator, novice drummers and even non-musicians can use hand drums and other similar world percussion instruments to play together in groups. Often the purpose of these drum circles is less about creating a performance and more about the relaxation and camaraderie that recreational music making involves.

Product Lines

The percussion market can be loosely categorized into several areas. These include combo, orchestral, marching, and world percussion. Each of these reflect different performance venues and musical styles, but there is certainly crossover with different instruments into any number of these areas.

Combo Percussion
The combo percussion market is clearly the largest and is centered around the drum set. This instrument at its basic form consists of: a snare drum, a bass drum played with a kick pedal, two small mounted toms attached to the bass drum, a larger floor tom, a set of hi-hat cymbals with a stand, a crash cymbal and a larger ride cymbal each with stands. Additionally, the drummer is seated on a stool or "throne". From this fundamental set, there is truly a limitless set of permutations and combinations adding additional drums,

cymbals, and mounted hand percussion or "toys". As these sets continued to grow, stronger hardware was developed and in some cases, "rack systems" were employed to suspend the additional drums and cymbals around the musician. Just assembling these Erector sets for each gig often takes an army of roadies, but the end result can truly be an impressive work of art! Of course, being able to actually play all of these simultaneously is another story as well. For some purists, the simpler the set the better and can even be a reflection of the musical talent of the percussionist; being able to get the most out of the least.

Newer to the combo market has been the advent of the electronic drum kit. These consist of a series of rubber pads or "triggers" that are mounted in the same general configuration as a traditional set's drums and cymbals. However, instead of an acoustic sound generated from hitting a drum head, the sound is generated through an electronic module that is connected to the triggers. This sound module or "brain" contains a variety of sampled drum and cymbal sounds that are then triggered when a musician hits the pad. These sets are virtually silent to the player until the module is connected to a PA source and amplified to the audience. With headphones the drummer can practice in near silence. With different sampled sounds, the musician can modify the sound of the set to mimic any number of acoustic sets that have been sampled.

Orchestral Percussion
This market, while smaller than the combo market, consists of some of the most expensive instruments in the percussion family. Instruments in this segment are used for more classical literature and are found in orchestras, concert bands, and wind ensembles. While some of these instrument are un-pitched, such as fine snare drums or concert toms, much of the larger instruments are pitched.

Some of the more common keyboard mallet instruments include concert bells, xylophones, vibraphones, and marimbas. These instruments are laid out to resemble the piano keyboard, but are played with mallets made from hard plastic, yarn, cord, rubber, or even occasionally brass. Similarly organized are concert chimes whose chrome or brass tubes are stuck with a rawhide or plastic hammer. Also part of the pitched orchestral percussion family are the timpani drums (kettle drums) which have a pedal mechanism to change the pitch of the drum head. These are organized as sets or two or four to cover their full pitch range.

Much of this family has changed very minimally over the years, although there has been a movement to substitute some of the more expensive and exotic woods (such as rosewood) with synthetic options. Still, the rather traditional nature of the music that is played also drives very little change for the orchestral percussionist.

Marching Percussion

While originally developed for its military use, marching percussion has perhaps evolved more than any other family. As the parade use migrated from the battlefield to main street, the purpose remained the same; to carry basic percussion instruments by the musician while performing. The three primary drums used in marching percussion are the snare drum, the bass drum (which can come in a plethora of sizes), and tuned tom drums (from trios to sextets).

Originally these drums were carried by a series of fabric slings. Snare drums were played off to the side and a leg brace provided stability. Use of slings were later replaced by aluminum carriers which allowed the drums to be positioned in front of the player. These carriers greatly added to the comfort of the player and could be held in place for extended periods. Today these very sophisticated drum carriers can be adjusted for both the size of the drum and the size of the musician for maximum comfort and mobility.

The Music Products Industry

As drum and bugle corps became more and more prevalent in the 1980s there was a continuous move to try to tighten the snare drum batter heads to achieve an extremely dry, high-pitched snap rather than the washy sound of a traditional snare. To achieve this, drum line directors began using batter heads made from woven Kevlar instead of standard polymers. While this gave the sound desired when cranked down to near concrete hardness, the drum shells would break before the head would give out. After all, these heads were made of the same materials as bullet proof vests!

To combat this problem, drum manufacturers redesigned the tensioning systems, redirecting the pressure from the drum lugs to the reinforced steel hoops. This "free floating" design has now become the standard for most marching snare drums, allowing for maximum strength without adding to the overall weight of the drum.

World Percussion
Perhaps the strongest growth in the percussion market in the past two decades has been in the world percussion area. As globalization of markets continue, the influence of different cultures has become very significant. Led by companies such as Remo, Toca, and Tycoon, many instruments once unique to specific regions of the world are now being incorporated into popular music.

Most of the world percussion instruments are played with the musician's hands and as such can be relatively easy to learn. This has led to the development of "drum circles". Often used simply as a form of recreational music making, participants gather in a circle led by a facilitator and develop intricate rhythm patterns and feed off of the energy of the other players.

Sales and Marketing Strategies

Much like the Pro Audio Combo market, the percussion business relies extensively on lesson instruction and artist endorsements. Depending on the sub-category of percussion instruments, the sales strategies can vary greatly. Generally speaking, lesson instruction for orchestral and marching percussion begins in the school band room. Students usually begin with simple lessons on just the snare drum and slowly add additional instruments and techniques. While some students may supplement with lessons outside of school, most often the instruction is from classroom teachers or adjunct clinicians such as drum line instructors. Combo percussionists that play primarily on drumsets often have little in-school instruction. Rather, these players will either take lessons from a music store, a studio, or simply try to go it alone. Online instructional videos have become more prominent, especially for beginning hobbyists. Stores that capitalize on converting these beginners into weekly students often win customers for a lifetime.

Combo Percussion
Endorsements from the pop market are key ingredients to marketing and brand development for combo percussion. Consisting primarily of drum set sales, manufacturers look for the newest, hottest stars to be photographed behind their sets. Adding to this, most rock drummers do not consider their career complete until they have a custom drumstick manufactured under their name. All of these endorsements work much in the same way as they do in the PAC market. Often endorsements are compensated in the form of either free gear or significant product discounts. For larger artists, additional compensation may be arranged, but usually it is limited. They are, however, solicited for new design ideas and general research and development. Brand loyalty based on endorsing artists can often create a lifetime customer for the manufacturer.

The Music Products Industry

Orchestral Percussion

While you may see an occasional endorsing artist for orchestra percussion instruments, they are pretty limited. Partly, due to the relative obscurity of these artists, they simply do not have the household names attached that their rock 'n roll counterparts do. The largest market for this product sub-category tends to be the educational market. So, as we will see when discussing the school service market, the school band instrument retailers are instrumental in marketing specific brands. The educational road reps often play a huge role in suggesting appropriate products based on the budget constraints and usage requirements for the school.

Marching Percussion

As discussed earlier, the marching percussion category has seen more design innovations and redevelopment than any other area of drums. The push for this came from its greatest influencers, the drum and bugle corps. For those unfamiliar with these groups, drum corps recruit late high school age and college students to spend a summer learning marching drill and music to be showcased in competitive shows across the country. To weather the grueling travel and outside use, the instruments must be both extremely durable and lightweight. While the majority of marching percussion is purchased by the school market, it is these corps that act as the most important endorsers. Often the drums that a winning corp marches in a season can boost sales significantly for that brand. Unlike other endorsing artists, drum corps usually get their drum lines free to use. Upon completion of the summer season, the used drums are marketed by the manufacturer and sold through a local dealer to high schools or college programs.

World Percussion

Even though many of the actual instruments in this category equate to some of the most ancient drums, it is only in the last few years that these instruments have found a home in today's market. There are few endorsing artists for these and marketing consists of drum circle development in both schools

44

and community organizations. The success of this product category can be attributed to the training of drum circle facilitators. Many school music educators have recently focused their additional training in this area as this has become a popular educational tool for the general music classroom.

Supplier-Dealer Chain

While dealer franchises exist in the percussion segment, they tend to be less common and much less restrictive than its PAC counterparts. Some of the larger manufacturers such as Yamaha and Pearl will have dealer agreements that require a minimum representation of the product line and have some territorial restrictions. The majority of the market tends to open to having multiple dealers in an area with sometimes only minimal buy-ins. The extremely wide array of products that fall into the percussion market translates into a huge number of different suppliers. Some of these suppliers act as the manufacturer of the actual instruments, but many others simply act as importers or distributors.

Financing

Similar to the PAC market, financing options for the retailer may be somewhat restrictive. The real muscle for arranging extended credit with suppliers often simply comes down to the buying power of the retailer and its credit-worthiness in the industry. Companies with long histories of successful purchasing are much more likely to arrange for financing terms with their suppliers. The most successful at achieving these terms are either large, big-box merchandisers or school music dealers. Less likely is the small boutique combo shops or percussion specialty stores.

Because some of the percussion products cross over to the school band instrument market, these dealers have financing terms in place already. We will see in the next chapter that these educational dealers can often purchase instruments from the manufacturers and not pay for them for nearly half of a year. This process allows for rental programs to exist where payments to the dealer come in small, incremental installments.

Additionally, items such as marching drum lines or large concert percussion items are often leased to the school. At a minimum it usually takes several months for a school to make their payments to the dealer. Having some flexibility for repayment to the vendor is critical, as these can often translate into purchases in the tens of thousands of dollars; enough to bankrupt an average music dealer.

Pricing Structure

Pricing structures for the percussion market tend to differ between the four product areas. Combo percussion, such as drum sets and cymbals, tend to follow the same MAP policies seen with the guitar market. Although once dominated by the large percussion manufacturers, today we find many off-shore branded drum sets at a relatively low cost of entry that may or may not be MAP protected. The drum sets sold by the major manufacturers, especially those in their upper tier quality lines, are MAP protected and usually franchised. Cymbals, while actually considered an "accessory" item in the industry, may also have pricing protection to insure value in the consumer's mind and to protect margins. Cymbals can sometimes be as valuable as the entire drum set and thus are treated differently than most accessories. They may even have franchise restrictions placed for distribution. But, most-often they are simply price protected.

Orchestral and marching percussion are marketed quite differently and have different pricing structures than their combo counterparts. Since these instruments are almost exclusively purchased by institutions (such as schools, symphonies, etc.) rather than by individuals, there are generally no MAP prices. Instead, these instruments are usually priced through a competitive bid basis. Rather than determining a bid price by calculating a discount from its list price, these instruments are priced by taking their cost and adding a percentage for profit and freight charges. Often these margins may be as little as 5 or 10 percent above cost, leaving very little profit margin for the retailers. However, these bids often involve high dollar instruments or large quantities of equipment such as entire drum lines. So, what is lost in margin is made up in quantity. Frankly, the purpose of a retailer trying to win a competitive bid for orchestral or marching percussion is more about insuring loyalty to the school music dealer than it is about making profit. The percussion manufacturer stands to gain much more on these sales. More on this later as we discuss the school market.

Finally, the world percussion market is treated much more like the accessory business and often has little pricing protection. The margins on these items can be quite high, however, and the industry has seen substantial growth in this area. Items such as congas, djembes, or tubanos can fetch a pretty penny. Major brands such as Remo and Latin Percussion (owned by DW Drums) have very deep inventory lines for world percussion. However, the market has many other players and consumers often do not have the strong brand loyalty we see in other product areas. This allows retailers more profit opportunities than seen in some of the other percussion market segments.

Future

The percussion market is one of the very oldest in the music industry. Interestingly, the future tends to be moving in two directions. The digital age has left its mark on the percussion industry to some extent as digital drum sets have seen growth over the years. However, that growth has now plateaued as many percussionists prefer the sound and feel of an acoustic instrument. Simultaneously, the industry has reached back to its earliest roots in search of some of the most historic and primitive instruments. As the industry continues to take on a more global characteristic this part of the percussion market will probably continue to expand.

One of the major challenges to the percussion market has plagued other markets as well. Today there is a strong focus in pop music on vocalists, but very little on the band backing them...if there is any band at all. Lost is the "Ringo effect" caused by musical "heroes" featured in major acts. Many of today's pop artists do not actually play an instrument and thus, do not inspire young musicians to take up playing one. This is a challenge that the industry must address to strengthen lagging drumset sales as well as other areas including the electric guitar market.

Another challenge for the percussion market is to find a way to tap into the female market. Traditionally, this product segment has been dominated by male instrumentalists. The guitar market has made great strides with this similar problem. The lagging drum market could use some help by focusing on this rather forgotten part of the population. Once again, the industry could sorely use a female drummer on the pop scene to be a mentor for young female percussionists worldwide!

None the less, it is everyone's secret fantasy to be a drummer, so there will be little worry that the percussion market will be continue to thrive well into the future.

Chapter 4

The Piano & Keyboard Market

The Marketplace

Almost every young child has head the words, "You need to take piano lessons!" Whether this has caused excitement or consternation, lessons on the piano are often the first instructions a young child receives when being introduced to the world of music. And, the reasons for this are valid. There is perhaps no other instrument that more completely encompasses the full musical realm. Its 88 note range is greater than any wind-blown instrument. Its music, represented on the grand staff, teaches not only note playing, but music theory. It can be both a solo instrument or played as part of an ensemble. Individual notes can outline a melody on one hand, while chords on the other provide its own accompaniment. Its voice can be heard in every style of music, from classical to jazz to rock 'n roll. In many ways, the piano is the ultimate musician's instrument!

Preceded by the harpsichord which used a keyed mechanism to pluck strings, the concept of the modern piano dates to the early part of the 18th century. A system of hammers that strike pitched strings and dampers that mute their vibrations allow a performer the ultimate musical control needed to play in both small and large venues. Indeed, its original name was "pianoforte", or "soft loud" which reflected this new mechanized system. Through the 1700s improvements to this concept changed, adopting modern wire manufacturing, redesigning the iron soundboard, and adding pedals to control

49

dampening. Today, simply shortened to "piano", the basic mechanics of this instrument remain fundamentally unchanged.

However unchanged the traditional acoustic piano maybe, technological influences have added to the menu of today's familiar instruments. Influenced by its early church origins, modern keyboards steal some of the same elements originally found on pipe organs. Using an elementary manual to activate the requested pitches, today's keyboards use digital technology to replicate sampled sounds of real acoustic pianos, pipe organs, harpsichords, and almost every other conceivable musical instrument.

While once found in nearly every household, the acoustic piano market has given way to many of these technological inventions. Digital pianos, that combine many of the conveniences and affordability of keyboards with the traditional mechanical action of acoustic pianos, have become commonplace in many homes. Small, but powerful, electronic keyboards are often the first instrument for budding pianists.

Acoustic piano technology has evolved very slowly over the last few hundred years. However, supercharged by first the transistor age and now the digital era, alternatives to acoustic pianos have eclipsed much of the traditional market. Four areas of development over the last 50 years or so have created a new landscape for this marketplace.

First, was the rise and fall of the home organ. Boosted by the technological developments of the Hammond Organ Company, the organ escaped from its traditional church venue and was thrust into nearly every home in America. While using early vacuum tube technology at its origins, home organs incorporated transistor technology which made them both cheap and reliable. Adding a spinning speaker horn known as a Leslie created the iconic sound associated with so many of the famous pop bands of the 70's. After all, what would Blood, Sweat, & Tears have been without Dick Halligans Hammond B-3 sound?

The Kimball home organ became ubiquitous to every living room in America. Others such as Wurlitzer and Hammond quickly joined suit. For piano dealers, it was a huge shot of capital for a rather mature, stale market. This would be short lived, however. Peaking in the late 1970s the home organ would soon be eclipsed by the portable keyboard.

While Hammond was dominating the organ market, Fender was branching out from its guitar origins to try to emulate an actual acoustic piano sound. The Rhodes piano, invented in the 1950s by Harold Rhodes, used a mechanical action similar to an acoustic piano to make contact with metal rods rather than traditional piano wire. These metal rods would then be amplified through the use of small, electromagnetic pickups, much like what was used in electric guitars. Leo Fender purchased the Rhodes Company in 1959 and began to market these to the professional musician market. Ray Manzarek, keyboardist for The Doors, made this sound an indelible part of rock n roll musical history.

A third historic player in the field was the pioneering efforts of Dr. Robert Moog. His experimental work with vacuum tube theremins and analog synthesizers would pave the way towards modern day keyboard technology. His Moog Synthesizer would be experimentally incorporated in modern pop music of the 1960s, including artists such as The Monkees and The Rolling Stones. While short-lived, the analog synthesizer would soon give way to the modern digital synthesizer due to the advent of the modern microprocessor.

The fourth and final chapter in the evolution of the modern keyboard marketplace would come with the incorporation of digital technology. This would both revolutionize the sounds produced and the portability of the devices. No longer limited by the sounds of an internal mechanism, external musical timbres could be sampled and replicated, allowing the instrument the freedom to take on virtually any audible sound. Perhaps no instrument was more iconic in bringing this to the pop music market than the Yamaha DX7 digital synthesizer keyboard introduced in 1983. Along with many other similar models introduced by Roland, Korg, and others, the Yamaha keyboard would become the signature sound of the 1980s and 90s pop music.

The importance of these technological developments would vastly affect the traditional acoustic piano market forever. Keyboards would continue to develop adding more and more features including touch sensitivity, on-board recording, and pre-sequenced rhythm tracks. The traditional market still demanded the advantages that its acoustic predecessor had always provided. New "digital piano" models would be developed that combined these features including weighted key action, sustain and sostenuto pedals, and full acoustic polyphony.

The acoustic piano market would be forever changed, but not gone. The way in which this market segment would be marketed would have to change to survive. The new technology is not going away, but needs to live symbiotically with its acoustic roots.

Customer Demographics

Like many instruments, the ideal time to begin to play is at a very young age. Unlike wind instruments found in school bands, piano students can begin as early as 5 years old. While they may not be able to yet reach the sustain pedals, the basics of keyboard fingering can be taught quite early.

Instilling the foundations of music through piano education has been around for over a hundred years. There is perhaps no more stereotyped image than a young student sitting at a piano with an elderly private teacher critically observing. Breaking this stereotype would become a matter of survival for this market segment. While the advent of keyboards and their use in pop bands would help, the piano market has taken a backseat in the industry where it once dominated.

One option in some school environments has been to create keyboard labs to teach classroom piano skills. This is done by connecting digital or portable keyboards together, using headphones for student's privacy, and allowing a lead instructor to listen to the individual progress of students.

Today, piano education is still at the root of all basic music education and is required in virtually every collegiate music program. Its inherent ability to showcase the entire concept of music theory under the players' very fingers would make pianists some of the most rounded of musicians. Virtually all composers use the piano as their basic tool for creating new music.

Going forward, the piano market has to instill the value of piano education with a new generation of students whose access to free time has never been in more demand. Whether it is competition with ball practice or video games, taking the time to learn an instrument such as piano is as much an exercise in patience as it is musicianship!

Product Lines

Like the name implies, the piano and keyboard market shares two main categories: traditional acoustic pianos and electronic digital keyboards. Each of these, however, have many subcategories that ready different market demographics.

For acoustic pianos, there are several primary body styles that are marketed quite differently. And, in addition to overall style, the finish and design become equally important factors. As many of these instruments sit very visibly in customer's homes, the cabinetry must fit the decor of the room in which they reside. In some ways, they become a part of the furniture. Consequently, different finishes and cabinet designs became part of the entire marketing package for a piano dealer. It is not uncommon for consumers to be as concerned with the piano's look as they do its sound!

One of the most familiar body styles is the grand piano. Built so that the soundboard and strings are constructed horizontally, these come in three customary sizes. Full concert grands, often found in recital halls, measure nine feet in length and are designed for maximum volume and acoustics. Smaller grands, sometimes known as parlor grands, are a few feet shorter. Baby grands, measuring a mere five and a half feet are often marketed for home use when a true display piece is desired.

Vertical pianos, as the name implies, are oriented so that the soundboard and strings sit vertically. The largest of these are uprights, where the full mechanical action sits above the actual keys. These have often been the choice of schools and other performance venues where sound volume is important. Smaller uprights such as consoles and studios have smaller cabinets and compress the action. The smallest, and for many years the most popular for homes with limited space, is the spinet. This uses a drop action which sits below the keyboard and has a very short profile.

Regardless of cabinet style, the acoustic piano is a sizable investment. This is due in part to the extreme amount of hand manufacturing work needed to build them. There can be as many as 10,000 parts in just the mechanical action alone! It is not surprising that electronic and digital alternatives would be opportune elements for upsetting the traditional acoustic market. Keyboards and their various relatives would now be the dominant players!

The keyboard market can really be separated into three main areas: organs, portable keyboards, and digital pianos. Likewise, these can be further separated based on styles and market demographics.

Organs

The organ market consists of institutional and home organs. As the name would imply, the institutional organ market sells primarily to venues with permanently installed fixtures. The most traditional, of course, would be churches. Still today, there is a market for traditional organs at many churches, but most of these have now incorporated many of the technologies found in modern keyboards. Few mechanical pipe organs are now installed, replaced by digital versions that have accurately sampled the various timbres of real pipe ranks. Organists can even pre-record their performances on their consoles to be replayed in their absence.

Adding pressure on this market subset is the influence of sacred pop music at many houses of worship. Today, more modern pop instruments such as guitars, drumsets, and electronic keyboards have replaced the once-traditional acoustic pipe organs of the past. This is a trend that is unlikely to reverse in the near future and sales in this segment have continued to decay over the last two decades.

As discussed earlier, the home organ market was once one of the hottest areas of the music industry. Its technological innovations would steal an enormous swath of market-share away from traditional acoustic pianos. However, this same technology would also be its demise as integrated circuits replaced tubes and hardwires. Its growth would also usher in the age of the portable electronic keyboard that was cheaper, more versatile, and far more portable. Today, the home organ market is a mere shadow of its once greatness and relies on marketing to an aging and vanishing elderly population.

The Music Products Industry

Portable Keyboards
As the digital age came into being in the early 1980s, so did the portable electronic keyboard. Feeding on the popularity ushered in by the use of home organs in non-traditional venues, such as the pop music scene, cheap sampling technology could make a small keyboard sound like almost any musical genre imaginable. These "voices" could be instantly accessed by the user or even linked together to create an ensemble sound with just one musician. Sophisticated features such as transposing options, pre-programmed rhythm tracks, and recording modules made even the simplest keyboards some of the most powerful instruments available.

Gone were the heavy electric pianos or awkward home organs. Keyboards could come in every size imaginable. The most common is 61, 76, or 88 keys, although some can have as few as 25 or 34. Some of the keyboards have traditional "box-shaped" piano keys, while others mimic the look of traditional organs. The "touch" can vary widely as well; some having only a lightly weighted feel, while others mimic the feel of the mechanical action of an acoustic piano.

While all have some type of on-board speaker system, their sound is often compromised by size and portability. Regardless, they almost always have a system to connect to both a PA system for amplification or a MIDI output for computer applications. Recording options vary greatly as well, with the larger models having a sizeable recording platform. Others depend on recording to a portable device such as a flash drive or similar firmware.

The portable keyboard market has also experienced a slow decline over the years except in the higher price points. The market has become quite saturated with many non-traditional outlets selling these simple musical devices. Downward price pressure has reduced the overall value of this subset of the market.

Digital Pianos

One of the most promising areas of the keyboard market in recent years has been the growth of digital piano sales. As a hybrid, a digital piano combines the electronic sampling found in portable electronic keyboards with the physical mechanics afforded by traditional acoustic pianos. Most notably is the addition of a more substantial framework that incorporates the three traditional sustain pedals. The full range of 88 keys are represented and have a mechanical action designed to simulate the historic hammered systems found in a piano. Musicians find that these not only accurately simulate the touch and feel of a traditional piano, but young players can more easily transition to an acoustic version at a later date.

Other features such as headphone jacks for silent practice, built in metronomes, and transposition options make the instrument ideal for young piano students. While not as portable as a smaller electronic keyboard, these digital pianos are far easier to move about than their heavier predecessors. Their digital processors never need tuning and the overall cost can be substantially cheaper than an acoustic version. That being said, there are many deluxe models that can rival the prices of some entry-level traditional pianos.

Sales and Marketing Strategies

There is quite the dichotomy in sales strategies between acoustic pianos and portable keyboards. The latter is similar to other parts of the music industry. Price points, features, and portability often weigh heavily on the final choice. In any case, keyboard sales tend to involve a shorter sales cycle and the overall turn of the inventory is significantly shorter. It is not unusual to see 3 or 4 inventory turns in a given sales year for the portable keyboard market.

Acoustic pianos generally require a longer sales process. The very cost and size of the instrument requires a more profound decision for most consumers. Consequently, the turn on inventory tends to be significantly slower than its electronic counterparts. For spinets and smaller home pianos, dealers usually turn their inventory only twice during a year. And, for grand pianos, this ratio goes down to one. Added to this is the fact that an acoustic piano is built to last. It is not uncommon for a piano that is periodically serviced to last 50 to 75 years, so the entry into the market for a consumer maybe a single lifetime event!

To promote activity in the acoustic market, dealers employ a variety of strategies. Lessons, both group and private, have long since been a part of their offering. After all, it does little good to own a $5000 piano and not be able to play it. For many years it was customary for families to purchase a piano for their home so that all of their children could take piano lessons and practice. The arrival of digital options has eroded much of this entry market. And, while the initial assumption is that students would later graduate to their acoustic siblings, fewer than 10% of children who start on piano continue. Often, these later, bigger purchases never materialize.

Another strategy mirrors that used in the band and orchestra market. College sampler programs allow dealers to provide acoustic pianos to university music departments for use in their practice or performance areas at no charge to the school. One caveat is that the college has to agree to an on-site piano "clearance sale" at the conclusion of the school year. These lightly "used" pianos could be marketed to the general public or even the music students themselves as bargains. The manufacturer would give the dealer significantly long repayment terms, understanding that this inventory would not be available for sale until the end of the school season.

This same kind of special sale outside of the traditional piano store showroom is repeated with "inventory reduction sales" or "truckload sales" brought in to large markets for a limited time. Sometimes sponsored in reality by a local dealer, but more often an event created by a piano manufacturer, these limited sales often enlist some of the top sales people from around the country. By sponsoring these events, piano manufacturers can create a sense of urgency with the consumer and often close the deal in one weekend instead of a lengthy incubation process.

The piano market requires expertly polished sales skills to succeed. Talented salespeople will spend a long time developing a relationship with the customer, take time to explain the entire manufacturing process, and build value in the product before ever demonstrating a particular piano. This is especially important when selling the higher end options such as grand pianos. Experienced piano salespeople are few and far between, but can earn large commissions on the larger tickets. Keeping these masters in a decaying market segment has been problematic as the same skills used to sell a Steinway grand could be employed to sell a Jaguar automobile.

Supplier-Dealer Chain

Establishing a dealer agreement for a piano franchise is not unlike other parts of the industry, but due to the limited market the territorial restrictions may be more pronounced. Manufacturers will protect established dealers who have proven sales histories and established good credit. Where once their might have been a dozen music dealers in a given town carrying acoustic pianos, today there may only be one or two.

An initial master order may be required for new dealers that represents the full line offered by the manufacturer. Reorders for established dealers will be negotiated based on both the market size and the sales history of the company. While there may be no specific minimum order to keep the franchise, savvy retailers will negotiate favorable terms with the vendor. Often these terms not only include price, but freight charges and repayment terms. As you might expect, freight for the acoustic piano market is a sizeable issue. Freight allowances given by the manufacturer to take larger orders fall directly to the bottom line for the dealers but also adds the burden of higher inventory totals.

Freight allowances may also apply to the keyboard market, but only when significant quantities are ordered and only for the newest models. Terms are rarely more than standard 30 days, although quick pay discounts may apply. Territorial restrictions are much looser, if they exist at all. It is not uncommon to find the same keyboard marketed in many music stores within the same town and even sold at non-traditional big box outlets. Also, internet sales generally have no territorial restrictions, so competition can be fierce.

Financing

One of the largest obstacles to the acoustic piano market is the substantial cost of the inventory. Given a product with a significantly slow turn ratio and a very expensive net cost, piano dealers are often crushed under the weight of their own inventory. Not unlike an auto dealership, piano dealers are presented with the challenge of keeping their showrooms full; representing options including model sizes, color finishes, and cabinet styles. To do this requires a substantial outlay of capital which often stretches beyond the means of an average dealer.

Recognizing this, outside **floor planning** is often arranged by the manufacturer either through an independent **factoring company** or a wholly owned financial subsidiary. Effectively, the retailer enters into a purchasing floor plan agreement with the piano manufacturer. Delivery of the inventory is taken and the dealer has 90 days before repayment must begin. At that point, any inventory remaining unsold is subject to a 10% per month **curtailment** payment to the financial institution until the net invoice is satisfied. Interest factors for the lender are built into the curtailment to pay for the cost of the capital.

If a piano is sold under the floor plan agreement, immediate repayment to the financier must occur for that unit. Periodic audits by the lending institution insure that the inventory claimed on the books is indeed still in the showroom and that capital from sold pianos didn't go to pay other expenses first.

Obviously, dealers that are able to finance most of their inventory without the help of a factoring company are able to retain more of the profits from the sale of their inventory than those that don't. Long established dealers with a history of solid fiscal management can achieve this given solid long-term fiscal planning. However, even the most savvy retailers can quickly find themselves in a cash crunch if sales begin to slow.

Financing can also be a factor for the consumers. Due to the high cost of entry for acoustic pianos, customers will frequently need to spread the payments out over a matter of months or even years. After all, a larger piano's price can often rival that of a small car! To expedite these sales, dealers often establish working relationships with local banks or factoring companies. Consumers with qualified credit can arrange for financing within the confines of the dealership. Another option for a piano dealer is to **carry the paper** internally. This takes a sizable cash fund for the dealer and transfers the risk to the dealer in the case of default. However, for shorter term financing, usually six months or less, this can be an option; especially if the dealer has elongated terms with the manufacturer for repayment.

Pricing Structure

Pricing for the portable keyboard market tends to vary from very low end models that are designed as disposable goods, to models that rival their acoustic counterparts. Digital pianos can often be as expensive as standard spinet acoustics. Pioneered in part by Yamaha and Kawai, acoustic pianos that have digital technology installed have married the two generations together. Modeled after the earliest player pianos that relied on paper cylinders to replay music without the performer, these instruments use hard disks or programmed flash drives to create a similar experience.

Generally, the standard net price to a dealer is 50% off of MSRP, but this can vary depending on the model and size of the order. There are generally no MAP prices enforced for acoustic pianos. Due to the sizable cost of the instruments, there is almost always a bit of horse trading that occurs between the dealer and the consumer. Also, these items are not realistically marketed on the internet, so the need for price policing is minimal.

Typically, the dealer will attempt to achieve about a 30% margin when all is said and done. Anything less than this leaves little room to pay for the expense of financing such a weighty inventory and for other ancillary services that may be included in the sale. Traditionally, a single complimentary piano tuning done on site at the customer's residence is part of the package. Delivery options may be included gratis or billed separately.

Sometimes a dealer's biggest competition may simply be the used or rebuilt market in its territory. The opportunity to take in used pianos and rebuild them can be another source of income, but can take a sizeable shop and employee pool to get this done.

Portable keyboards sales are handled much more like the PAC market. MAP pricing is customary and generally establishes the street price for the product. Margins on these can vary but need to be somewhat higher to make up for their lower price point. The difficulty in handling the electronic brethren is that often the technological changes to the models happen so frequently that the store stock can quickly become obsolete. It is not uncommon for models to change yearly. As such, any MAP protection is usually limited to the first few months after a model is released, and it is immediately removed once a new model is planned. This allows for the market to quickly flush out the old inventory at rock bottom prices and keep newer models from cannibalizing dead stock.

Keeping the price affordable for acoustic pianos has been an ongoing challenge in the industry. Like so many other markets, manufacturing for most companies has moved offshore. Steinway remains as one of the only piano companies whose manufacturing still exists in the United States. Gone are many of the U.S. companies that used to dominate the market. In fact, the Kimball Company, once a leader in acoustic pianos, transitioned to just making furniture and left the music business entirely. After all, the art of making a piano involves a great deal of woodworking!

Future

Indeed, the acoustic piano market has been in a slow, steady decline for a century. The most pianos sold in the United States was 364,500 and that was back in 1909! Today that number has receded to around 35,000 annually. Erosion from the digital age combined with competing interests bombarded towards today's youth have made the piano market a mere image of its once glorious days.

The likely survivors will include music stores that are able to include a mix of instruments rather than simply acoustic pianos. In addition to portable keyboards and digital pianos, strong dealers may represent multiple industry products segments. Regardless, the piano market continues to reinvent itself by combining the technological advancements of recent years with its historic roots as one of the industry's most important musical icons.

The Music Products Industry

Carl Anderson

Chapter 5

The School Band & Orchestra Instrument Market

The Marketplace

For anyone who has ever seen the famous Broadway show, "*Musicman!*", you have already been introduced to the basic concept of the school band and orchestra instrument market. While this timeless classic may seem a bit campy and dated by today's standards, it is not nearly as outdated of a business model as it may first appear. In the story, a peddler of musical wares travels from town to town hawking the concept of learning music as a way to keep young kids from getting into trouble…"And there will be trouble…right here in River City!" As Professor Harold Hill's marketing plan, he enters a town, identifies a problem (young kids with idle time on their hands), and offers a solution...Music! After taking orders from townsfolk for band instruments, Professor Hill's scheme is to escape to the next town before the public discovers that they are missing the one key ingredient. No one is there to teach them to read music and actually play the instruments! Hence, the creation of the "Think System".

This is not to suggest that the band and orchestra instrument segment of the industry is in anyway reflective of Professor Hill's unscrupulous ways. To the contrary, this industry segment has probably done more to promote music education than nearly any other segment. Rather than employing the

65

The Music Products Industry

"Think System", school music retailers worked very hard in the 50's and 60's to instill instrumental music education into the public school systems around the country.

However, there are some positive similarities to the "Musicman" model that can't be ignored. First, it has always fallen to the school music retailer to help create a "need" for the product. Representatives from the retailers traditionally have assisted band and orchestra directors in recruiting young students into the instrumental music programs. With the same promise of being on stage or parading down the street, students are inspired to take up their music studies with a shiny new clarinet or trombone (or perhaps 76 of them!).

Second, the retailer sets up shop, often right in the school music room, to rent or sell band and orchestra instruments to be tried by the students. Finally, the instruments are delivered for their first day of band or orchestra with the promise of wonderful music ahead of them. Unlike Professor Hill, our modern day retail road reps continue to service the schools, often through weekly visits, to assist with further music and accessories needs or to repair and service the instruments in use.

Customer Demographics

In some ways the band and orchestra (B&O) market is a little trickier than some. Paramount to this is the fact that the school market has actually three customers at work for every sale. Obviously, the student is the ultimate consumer of the product and often represents the strongest proponent of the purchase or rental...at least until the shine of the new instrument begins to dull and the realization that hours of practice are required for ultimate success.

The second consumer in the equation is the parent who will represent the financial element. In order to secure their trust, there must be value equated not only to the instrument, but to the whole educational process. And, that is where the third element comes in. The instrumental music teacher becomes an additional side of the sales triangle, both promoting their program and endorsing the representative retailer and specific brands or models they carry. This synergistic model is at the heart of the school music market.

In a perfect system, there is a synergy of trust. The student trusts the music teacher that they will learn how to play an instrument. The teacher trusts the music store to provide quality, working instruments at a reasonable price. And the parents trust the teacher to endorse one or more retailers as their preferred dealer(s) for products the parents often know very little about.

If any one of these trusts are broken, the sales cycle falters. If a teacher does a poor job at teaching and retaining students, the students' music education is hurt, the retailer gets back a rental return, and the parents are out money. If the parents do not trust the retailer or the educator's endorsement and purchase outside of the sales triangle, the student is often left with a poor quality instrument, the retailer loses out on a sale, and the students cannot excel. If the retailer does not provide a satisfactory product or rental program, parents do not get value for their money, the educators do not have the proper tools to create students who learn music, and the future of the school's music program is a risk. It is all built on equal trust

Education systems vary, but usually the starting age for band instruments is around 5th grade or 10 years of age. Orchestral programs often start a year earlier, partly to get a jump on recruiting over their band counterparts. To a fifth grader, orchestra instruments sometimes seem less glamorous. They are not seen in parades, marching band contests, football games, or jazz ensembles. So, educators try to stack the deck a bit by starting earlier. In some cases this works and students fall in love with playing violin or cello, but too often the students lose interest and see orchestral programs as simply "pre-band". Programs where both band and orchestra are offered at the same age level may lose a little to one another, but frankly often do better with retention in the long run.

Of course, studying to play a string instrument does not have to wait until school age. Unlike band instruments, orchestra instruments easily come in different sizes. Everything is cut down to scale and violins can be as small as a 1/16th violin, designed for students as young as three years of age! Because of the different acoustic properties of band instruments, especially winds, students must wait until they can handle an "adult" sized instrument, which is usually around 9 or 10 years of age.

Product Lines

When the band and orchestra instrument market began to gain legs, there were quite a few American owned companies that populated the market. Legendary names have stood the test of time, but more recently have been consolidated and purchased by only a few remaining large companies.

Some of the most significant band instrument companies included C. G. Conn located in Elkhart, Indiana noted for its brass and later woodwinds under the Artley name. King, which grew out of the H.N. White company, was located in Eastlake, Ohio and also specialized in brass until the Armstrong line of woodwinds became part of its brand. Holton and Leblanc were in Kenosha, Wisconsin, specializing in brass and woodwinds respectively. Vincent Bach originally started in Mt. Vernon, New York before later migrating to Elkhart, and became synonymous with trumpets and trombones. Gemeinhardt Flutes also settled in the northern Indiana town of Elkhart which became somewhat known as the band instrument capital of the world. Many of these companies settled in the midwest because the labor pool that was created from this unique industry was well-established and workers migrated back and forth to various companies. Other companies such as E.K. Blessing, Benge, Olds, Schilke, and many others helped to establish the U.S. Market.

Some foreign companies also played a significant role in the market development. Selmer was established in Paris, France and later created a partnership distribution line in the U.S. that was eventually connected to the Bach company. Buffet was also a French company noted for its fine line of clarinets. Late to the game was Yamaha in Japan. Started originally as a company that made reed organs, it grew quickly and in the 1960s added a band instrument line. Until the late 1990s Yamaha had a manufacturing plant in Grand Rapids, Michigan to produce its student line of instruments for the U.S. market, but retreated from that market as U.S. labor grew too expensive relative to Asian production. Its U.S. headquarters is, however, in Buena Park, California. Another late-comer to the party was KHS and its Jupiter brand of instruments. This Taiwanese company originally started manufacturing bicycles and got into the musical instrument business much later. The instrument division of KHS is now located in Mt. Juliet, Tennessee, just outside of Nashville. Other companies such as Courtois in

France and Boosey & Hawkes from Great Britain have been major players, especially in the foreign markets.

Today's U.S. market is not nearly as fractured as it once was. Only a handful of companies dominate the field and much of the actual production is not on American soil. This is especially true for the lower end, student models. Conn-Selmer is still headquartered in Elkhart, IN but now is a conglomeration of many brands including: Conn, Artley, Armstrong, King, Holton, LeBlanc, Yanagasawa, Ludwig, Musser, and Sheryl & Roth. Yamaha is a huge player and collectively is the largest musical instrument maker in the world. Gemeinhardt Flutes is now owned by a Taiwanese company known as Angel Industries after having been sold by a group of investment bankers who owned the company under the Gemstone name. Its parts are mostly made in its original Elkhart facility, but the flutes are assembled overseas to capitalize on cheaper labor. Others, such as Schilke, Cannonball, E.K. Blessing continue to round out the market.

Sales and Marketing Strategies

As stated earlier, the school band and orchestra market is more dependent on market development than many other industry segments. The close ties that both retailers and their related manufacturers can make to both the school districts and their music educators are paramount to their eventual success. Recruiting strategies for retailers often involve road reps actually entering the public and private schools and demonstrating the instruments to young children. Once the demand for the product is established, the vast majority of school music dealers use some sort of rental program to allow students to test the waters before making a final purchase commitment.

There are two very common sales programs that retailers use with their instrument rental programs. While there are many variations, they can be boiled down to either a "**lease pool**" concept or a "**rent to own**" strategy. Each has certain advantages to the retailer and often the choice boils down to the financial strength of the company and the market pressures from competing retailers.

Lease Pool
In a "lease pool" strategy the music retailer will purchase an initial cache of lease-only instruments that can be categorized as capital assets. As such, these instruments can be depreciated over time by the business with some clear tax advantages. The lease pool instruments can be rented to customers on a monthly basis, but as capital assets they generally can never be sold. Rental programs vary widely, but often allow customers to accrue at least a portion of this rental money toward the purchase of an actual salable instrument. Often, there is a ceiling to the number of months that can have monies apply. At some point, the business will send a reminder to the customer that they can now turn in their rental instrument and apply some or all of this rental money towards the purchase of a new instrument.

The advantages of this style of program are many. First, the business can take the depreciation of the asset pool over time or all at once and show this as an expense against overall profits. Second, the music store does not actually purchase salable inventory until it knows for sure that the sale will be consummated, thus reducing the potential for rental returns of actual inventory. The student's ultimate instrument will be a new instrument, which is often desirable for serious students. Finally, and most importantly, the retailer's financial outlay for inventory is limited to the one-time purchase of the lease pool, and only purchases new inventory with a solid commitment from the customer. This final commitment from the customer can create a purchase contract (rather than a reversible rental contract) that can be sold as a financial instrument for cash to a third party financier. This removes the collection problems often associated with long term financing and replenishes the retailer's cash reserves to replicate the transaction with the next customer. This is why younger, less financially stable retailers often start with this model.

This style of lease pool rental is not without its negatives, however. The lease pool looks great in the first few years. But, as instruments are rented out they begin to wear and cause maintenance problems. They also are not as shiny and inviting to customers...kind of like getting your big brother's hand-me-downs. This can affect a customer's perception of worth, not to mention the young child's pride of having his or her own shiny instrument. The biggest concern involves what in the industry is known as "**conversion rate**". This is the number of customers who, when they get the letter explaining that it is time to commit to purchasing an instrument, will actually sign a new contract or pay a balance in full. Generally, customers tend to shy away from making long term commitments to purchases, especially when it involves the often fickle interests of a 10-year old. This can become a problem for the educators as well when a child quits unexpectedly due to the parents not renewing the rental agreement. The other problem that this program creates is sporadic purchases from the manufacturer. This often means that retailers cannot leverage the best prices for instrument franchises. More on this later.

But, regardless of its negatives, this rental pool option is a solid choice for many retailers, especially ones that only seasonally enter the school market. It creates cash flow during the rental months without committing to stifling inventory levels. It also can work quite well in the string orchestra market where rental instruments are partial-sized and not really something a consumer wishes to purchase. After all, if the child starts at a young age, a parent could wind up owning a half dozen partial sized instruments by the time the child is in junior high.

Rent to Own

The second type of rental program is the "rent to own" style. The essence of this program also requires a large purchase of inventory. But, rather than this being a one-time purchase, the retailer is simply acquiring a season's worth of inventory all at once. These instruments are not part of a lease pool and thus are not depreciable capital assets. Instead, these are simply normal inventory that can be sold at will without strings attached (pardon the pun). The instruments are rented on a monthly basis and usually the rental money applies directly to the actual instrument being rented. As students discontinue and stop renting, these "**rental returns**" are placed back into inventory to be rented at a lower price. There is a myriad of variations and pricing strategies associated with this style of rental.

The advantages of this style of program are many. First, there is no conversion letter, as the consumer is basically buying the initial instrument with which they began. As such, there is little risk of customers discontinuing because of some long-term commitment imposed by the dealer. Second, the instruments always tend to be in better shape because they are constantly being replenished with new inventory every year. While some of the inventory may be "rental returns", by the second or third time the instrument is rented the odds are good that one will eventually stick as a purchase. Rental returns are basically used instruments that are often very desirable for customers looking for a lower price option both for rental or simple purchase.

The most significant disadvantage of the rent-to-own program is the often staggering cost of the initial outlay each year. Because low rental rates often mean that it can take many years for an instrument to be paid off, a retailer must continue to carry these customers' financing while repurchasing inventory for the next season. This can often simply be too much cash for younger retailers to absorb. Still, for the retailer, this method has often translated into much greater long-term profits.

The tax consequences of this process are often interesting as well. While this can vary from state to state, most rent-to-own programs allow taxes to be collected on receivables rather than the upfront price of the instrument, since there is a certain percentage of these instruments that will be returned unsold. Basically, sales tax is paid on the difference between what the sale price of the instrument was at the beginning of the rental and the balance remaining on the instrument when it is returned.

School Bids & Leases
A final marketing strategy for school band and orchestra retailers is to sell the instruments directly to the school systems. Care needs to be taken when encouraging schools to be in the business of owning instruments traditionally purchased by consumers. At first glance, this may seem like a reasonable strategy, especially in economically challenged communities. These good intentions often backfire, however. When parents and students do not have a financial commitment in the process, it often translates to significantly lower retention rates. After all, the shine and glamor of a new instrument often tarnishes once the concept of practicing is introduced. Parents that have a significant financial investment in the process will often encourage, or even insist, that their children stick to their commitment. All directors face this plateau period of growth with young students and school owned instruments can simply make it "too easy" to quit. Additionally, students often do not care for instruments that are not their "own" and significant damage is done annually to school-owned inventory with little or no consequences to the child or their parents.

However, there are many instances when it makes much more sense for the school or institution to purchase certain instruments. Large and expensive "background instruments" such as tubas, bari-saxes, string basses, bass clarinets, and almost all concert and marching percussion are often owned by school districts or parents associations. The high price or seasonal use of some of these instruments make it impractical to be purchased by traditional consumers, unless they are professional musicians specializing on these instruments.

In such cases as these, either a bid purchase or lease option to the school is often in order. Schools generally purchase these larger and more expensive instruments at a significantly higher discount than offered to regular consumers. These bid prices are usually just 5-10% above cost, rather than discounted from a set list price. Knowing that the margin is so small to the retailer (rather than the manufacturer), many instrument makers will pass along an additional discount to the retailer on such bids to encourage their brand to be chosen for the bid. More on this later when we discuss retail financing....

When schools wish to purchase a significant quantity of these instruments at once, another option is a school lease. The "lease" moniker is a bit deceptive, as these transactions rarely have a "return" option component like a traditional rental contract. Rather, these are simply a way for schools to finance a large purchase over a sequence of fiscal school years, rather than having to pay all at once. Retailers may choose to finance this lease paper internally or pass along the contract obligation to a third party, often one affiliated with the manufacturer of the instruments on the lease. The choice here, once again, often boils down to the financial stability of the retailer to absorb the cost of the inventory while waiting several years to get paid. In any case, a finance charge is either added to the transaction or more often built into the lease installment price of the instruments to the school.

Leasing provides many advantages to the schools. First, the school is able to purchase all of their needed equipment at once. This is especially important when trying to match multiple instruments such as a drum line or timpani purchase. Second, the school is able to "lock in" to the current prices of the instruments rather than having them run the risk of inflation over subsequent purchasing years. Third, the school can spread the payments over several years when normally this price exceeds a typical annual school budget.

There are similar advantages for the retailer as well. By financing everything at once, the winning retailer will get the entire order, rather than risking it being bid out each subsequent year. If financing internally, the retailer can earn some interest money on carrying the paper over several years. A winning lease can also tie a school to a specific vendor for multiple years as lease payments are made.

Supplier-Dealer Chain

Like many of the product categories, the most common supplier/dealer relationship is established with a franchise agreement. Perhaps more so than others, band instrument manufacturers are quite picky about how saturated the market gets with their product line. Due to the significant investment and unique marketing strategies outlined earlier, vendors will make sure that new dealers are not competing too directly with other similar retailers. Criteria vary, but manufacturers will require retail dealers to purchase a minimum master order yearly that represents their entire line. So, if the vendor makes student, intermediate, and professional instruments, the dealer will need to purchase a sufficient quantity of products in each of these categories.

Manufacturers may have some other criteria in place as well before opening a retailer as a dealer. Such criteria often include having an on-site repair facility, traveling road reps, and a physical retail outlet. Most often these are to determine if the store is really a "school music dealer" or just an MI store wishing to jump into the school market seasonally.

Opening online dealers can get a bit stickier. Brick and mortar stores often oppose having an online presence competing in their market, especially since it is usually the in-school marketing approach by the physical retailer that has actually created the market demand. Yet, many manufacturers are unwilling to forgo the sheer volume of sales that an online dealer represents. While many brick and mortar stores also have an online sales presence, it is the solely-online stores that appear to feed off of the handiwork of the local stores. To combat this, some manufacturers have created special "proprietary" lines of instruments that can only be sold in stores with a physical location. While this in theory gives a brick and mortar a marketing edge, the reality is that many of these instruments are nothing more than repackaged versions of the standard instruments sold online.

There is also a dichotomy between the retailers and the manufacturers regarding product mix in the stores. Student line instruments usually represent the "bread and butter" of profit for the school music dealer. These are often sold at or near list price through a rental program or only marginally discounted for cash sales. These instruments are the most price-sensitive to the dealer and the retailer will often choose its franchise master orders based on which vendor's prices are the cheapest. Since there is often little differentiation between brands at this entry-level price point, it becomes a race to the bottom to be the cheapest. Cheaper prices mean more margin to the dealer and less to the manufacturer.

Conversely, it does not take substantially higher manufacturing costs to produce a "**step-up**" or premium brand instrument. While there is some added labor and parts, including fancier cases or finishes, manufacturers are able to establish significantly higher list prices on these instruments. As musicians advance as players, brand and model preference become much more important, and the manufacturers have been able to position themselves to be the "preferred" instrument to customers. Since these premium instruments are generally not sold through a lease program, their "street price" or "price to market" becomes highly sensitive to competition. While MAP (Minimum Advertised Pricing) has curtailed some of these pricing problems, margins for these instruments to the dealer are much smaller than they are for the manufacturer. Instrument makers pour a significant amount of money each year to establish and maintain this brand preference in the market.

All this is why nearly every manufacturer has student, intermediate, and professional models represented in their mix and insist that their franchised dealers carry some inventory of all of them. Retailers make their margins on the entry level instruments, but establish themselves as trusted dealers by also carrying the higher end products. The manufacturers make their margins on the higher end instruments, but make up the difference by selling in volume on the lower margin items.

College Samplers
These brand preferences are often influenced by private instructors or the music educators in the schools. To help establish these preferences, both manufacturers and retailers often assist collegiate music education majors by providing free instruments for education tech classes. These "**college sampler**" programs enable new instruments to be used by the college students as they learn to master all of the various instruments they must eventually teach.

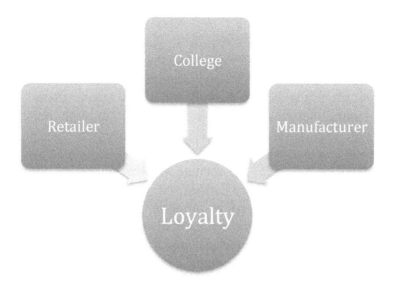

Through this program, the manufacturer ships instruments to the retailer to be delivered to the university. At the conclusion of the semester or school year of use, the instruments are returned to the dealer who is then billed for the instruments, usually with some extended dating terms and a discounted price since these will now be "used" inventory. These programs create a three-way win for all of the parties. The students and colleges do not have to pay for the use of the instruments. By introducing their instrument brand to the students, manufacturers begin to establish brand loyalty with the future educators. Finally, the retailers also create a relationship with the new educators in the hopes of future business once they land a teaching job.

Financing

Perhaps of all the music retail segments, the school market is the most seasonal. While the sales season is relatively short, usually only about 4-6 weeks, it is intense. The school sales season can also vary depending on the area of the country and is often referred to as the "**display season**" or the "**rental drive**". Many schools focus this recruiting drive during the first few weeks back to school in August and September. Other schools recruit at the end of the previous school year to establish a roster for the fall. Some of these spring recruitments will involve some pre-instruction through summer programs before school starts. However, many of these "extra" lessons have been eliminated through budget cuts.

Regardless of the time, the retailer must be prepared with a large volume of inventory before the recruiting season. In order for the manufacturers to properly provide this volume, intense forecasting is done by their district managers and as much pre-ordering is done as possible. This allows the manufacturers to manage production throughout their year and fill shipments in time for the retail outlets. For retailers with a large autumn selling season, orders are usually placed by February or March for shipment later in the spring. It is not uncommon for some vendors to run incentive specials for retailers to take delivery of inventory as early as November for use the following autumn. By doing this, the manufacturer is able to convert its "**inventory**" into an "**accounts receivable**", which can be a more-leveragable asset that can be used as collateral for financing. It is often advantageous to have this in place prior to ending their fiscal calendar year.

However, retailers would be crippled if they had to pay cash for shipments on inventory that cannot be sold or rented for nearly half a year or more. It is difficult enough to meet cash commitments for these payables when rental plans often mean a slow and relatively minimal cash flow to the dealer. Recognizing this dilemma, manufacturers often offer significantly long repayment terms to the dealers, sometimes stretching to nearly nine months for even the first installment payment. For most dealers this first payment would come at the end of September or October. These terms are known in the industry as "**fall dating**".

Customarily, these dating plans also come with incentives for early payments. That is, a discount can be taken if the invoice can be paid before the due date. These discounts for cash are found throughout the industry, but none more profound than the school market, where early pay can mean literally six months, rather than a few weeks found in other market segments. With the dating being so lengthy, the cash discounts may be staggered, giving higher and higher discounts for each earlier month.

While cash discounts may be nice for both the retailer and the manufacturer, they are often impossible on sizeable orders that are intended to be used through a rental program. Since the cash flow from consumers of such instruments are likely to be spread out for many months, or even years, the retailer must calculate a way to obtain financing for the payment of the master order invoice. The most likely candidate for such financing is the manufacturer itself, or a third party financier able to handle the "paper" for the retailer. In these cases, the retailer will pay an installment payment in October, and pay further installments every fiscal quarter at an increasing interest rate. This is why so many retailers offer their end consumers significant incentives to pay off the rental accounts in full and take ownership of the instruments. This allows a cash infusion to the dealer by spring so that financing obligations can be met to the manufacturer in time to begin the whole process over for the following year.

Professional and "step-up" instruments are usually not included in fall dating, but are often given up to 120 days to pay. These also usually have staggered and progressively larger cash discount incentives tied to early payments.

Large bid sales directly to schools are also subject to some financing help by the manufacturer. In these cases, the manufacturer recognizes that the retailer often must wait several months for schools to pay for such purchases as it works through budgetary and school board approval. To aid with this, 90 or 120 day terms may be afforded with similar cash payment discounts as the premium instrument purchases.

Controlling these cash payment terms can be some of the most important accounting work the retail dealer must do, as much of the school music market is not sold on a "cash" basis, but rather some kind of extended lease or rental plan as earlier described. Without proper controls in place, a single retail season can bankrupt a dealer even if, or sometimes because, sales are brisk! In the end, "Cash is King!"

Pricing Structure

Due to the rent to own nature of the school instrument business, it is one of the few market segments whose price is more closely tied to the "retail or list" prices suggested by the manufacturers. While pricing strategies vary drastically depending on the nature of the rental programs as described earlier, the student instruments are rarely tied to a Minimum Advertised Price (MAP) like more expensive, premium or "step-up" instruments might be. To understand this is to really understand the essence of the school market business. Customers are not simply buying an instrument. They are buying the opportunity for their student to participate in the school's instrumental music program.

Because of all of this, retailers really are not only in the merchandise business. They are virtually in the "insurance" and the "banking" business. While certainly not chartered as such, the retailer provides the essence of these two basic services to customers by creating a rental program and transferring the risk accordingly.

Essentially, the retailer is placing a bet against the customer in the same way an insurance company would. A customer who takes out automobile insurance is betting that they will have an accident and need to be compensated for their damages. The insurance company is basically betting that the driver will drive safely and it will do everything in its power to encourage that practice. The insurance premium reflects the value of that feeling of security. Essentially, the music retailer does the same thing. The parent assumes that playing music is a passing fancy and tries to avoid the "risk" of purchasing an instrument they might no longer need. The retailer, on the other hand, is assuming that the child will take an interest in music and will do everything in its power to encourage that, so that the instrument will eventually be purchased. The inflated price over what would be charged in a more traditional, non-returnable sale reflects the value of that "security" the customer feels.

Additionally, many rental programs have a "maintenance or repair" charge associated with the rental which covers any type of damage done to the instrument while in the child's hands as well as normal maintenance issues. This is more reflective of traditional insurance. However, retailers that "insure" an instrument against more traditional losses such as fire or theft run the risk of violating regulatory insurance charters. While occasionally done, this practice should be avoided.

The retailer also commonly acts as the banker to the customer. Even customers who are certain their child is the next musical prodigy may be unable to pay the entire price of an instrument up front, even at a discounted price. The rental strategy creates a quasi financing plan, to make an otherwise unaffordable instrument approachable to a diverse socioeconomic customer base. As such, retailers must use due diligence in screening even rental customers, as potential losses caused by delinquent customers can be staggering. It is often a complex process to repossess an instrument that is being used by a young student in a school environment. This shrinkage is inevitable to some extent, but a retailer is wise to price the merchandise accordingly to reflect this built-in loss.

This "banking" strategy within the rental plan may also include a finance charge as discussed earlier. This acts as both an incentive for customers to pay off the instrument before next year's master orders are due and as compensation to the retailer for "carrying the customer's financing" internally. Often these finance charges are significantly higher than the cost of capital in the financial markets, but once again reflect the risk that a retailer takes with often minimal customer credit screening.

Future

While in its infancy in the 1950's, the school instrument market is an aging business model. As such, retailers and manufacturers alike have had to adapt to market changes fueled by a global economy and a much more interconnected consumer base. While rural customers and schools were once dependent on a visiting retailer for access to supplies and information, the internet has broken down these dependencies. The retailers must constantly emphasize the service aspect of their businesses to compete.

The manufacturers who once were centered in Elkhart, Indiana and a handful of European music hubs now have production facilities all over the world. Increasingly, new companies with manufacturing plants in the Asian continent have grown substantially in both their size and viability. While once considered cheap knock-offs, some of these companies have had a substantial impact on the overall market and brought pricing pressure against some of the historic monoliths. Some of these downward pressures have called into question the need for the "insurance" and "banking" aspects, as consumers can more easily purchase these low cost instruments and assume the risk as a "disposable" product if the child changes his or her mind. However, these can also corrode music programs if inferior instruments are introduced into a school systems without due diligence by the music educator.

In any case, the school music market has remained a viable and very stable part of the music industry for decades. Perhaps this market, more than any, is dependent on our industry's music advocacy programs to make sure music stays as an integral part of our educational systems and creates music makers well into the future.

The Music Products Industry

Chapter 6

The Print Music Market

The Marketplace

While Professor Hill's "Think System" from the Music Man was much more reliant on young musicians improvising their way to success, centuries worth of more traditional teaching has created a universal language of musical notation. Dating back to the days even prior to the printing press, standard musical notation has been used as a way to preserve the creation of musical thoughts by a composer and disseminate it to the world. In fact, the very creation of the first printing press paved the way to modern copyright law as it became necessary to protect the musical intellectual property of the composer.

While this book is not the forum to fully discuss the changes in copyright law over the last century, and especially the last decade, it is important to understand that the strength of copyright is critically important to preserve this market segment. After all, the product is merely ink-smudges on a piece of paper if it is not backed by the protection of copyright.

The Music Products Industry

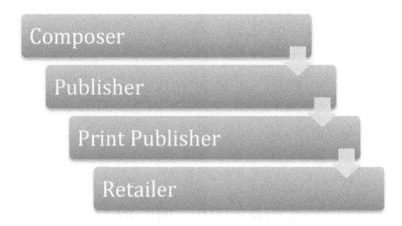

The print market consists really of a four-step process. First, the composer must write the piece of music. Second, the composer often allies with a traditional publisher that registers the piece with the Copyright Office and begins to find ways to exploit its use, that is, monetize the intellectual property by licensing it for various media. For many compositions this licensing involves a third player, the print publisher, which is basically a printing press that mass produces printed copies, markets these, and distributes them through their vast network of retail dealers.

The fourth and final step, then, is the retail dealer that handles sheet music that sells the product to the end-consuming musician.

One of the biggest challenges to each of the four steps involves the Pareto Principle. Vilfredo Pareto was a bean farmer in Italy who discovered that 80% of his yield of beans came from just 20% of his bean plants. As an economist he also realized that 80% of the farmland in Italy was owned by just 20% of the population. This same concept has been extrapolated into nearly every business. 80% of a business' revenues often come from just 20% of its clients, for example.

The Pareto Principle also is true in the music products industry where just 20% of the product tends to account for 80% of the sales. In the print music business, the actual figure tends to be more like 70/30, but the concept remains and presents a challenge for all four steps of the print music process.

70% of a composer's income come from just 30% of his/her titles. 70% of a publisher's sales come from just 30% of the works represented. 70% of a print publisher's sales also come from just 30% of the printed titles. And, of course, the retailer experiences the same issue with 70% of the revenue yielding from just 30% of the inventory. The rest of the inventory tapers off quickly in sales in what is known as the "long tail" in the sales chart.

The challenge for all of the parties involved is to determine what 30% will be the "winning titles". Short of a crystal ball, there is often little chance of knowing for sure. To be viable most publishers and retailers need to represent a bit of everything in their respective businesses. But this can come at a huge cost due to the characteristically slow turn ratio inherent to the print business. The long tail is often supported by the quicker moving sales of the hot sellers.

To protect the slower, classic titles from falling into total obscurity that an efficient capital market will almost always insure, several European countries enacted The Retail Price Maintenance Act. This law, which does not exist in the U.S., forces retailers to sell all titles at full retail even if they do not sell well. This artificially insure the protection of slow moving titles and effectively makes the more popular titles underwrite its poor brethren… a sort of socialism for print music, if you will.

The industry has weathered many technological changes that have both improved the quality and distribution of the product, but also challenged its sustainability. The simple office copy machine, which became commonplace in the 60s and 70s, paved the way for people to have access to instant copies. Once reserved to offset printing presses, these devices instantly allowed people the temptation to photocopy music from friends instead of purchasing it.

This same technology in its modern form is the **digital printing press**. This device has allowed publishers to preserve printed music in a digital form so that sheet music can be printed "on demand". Not only has this eliminated much of the music from being "out of print", but publishers are more willing to adopt riskier, avant garde submissions without the worry of stockpiling poor sellers.

Today, the advances of technology are disrupting much of the Pareto problem, allowing retailers to avoid costly extra stock by using digital downloads. Print publishers can take on riskier titles from publishers and composers without having to commit to large print production runs. Publishers or composers can even sell directly to consumers, bypassing the traditional retail model.

The technological revolution continues pushing the product directly into consumer's homes via websites that allow digital downloads. Like much of the Internet, the marketplace is full of both legal and illegal sites that allow this convenience. Going forward, this will continue to be a challenge for the industry, much like the recorded music industry struggled in the past. However, the industry consensus seems to be that print music will continue to be a viable market, if for no other reason that printing and binding larger works can be problematic in a home environment.

Customer Demographics

Like much of the music industry, the challenge to selling sheet music is creating a demand for it. Two factors affect this. First, the consumer must learn to actually read the notation for it to be valuable. Ironically, this sometimes requires the consumer to purchase a sheet music method book to become educated with the notation and open the gateway to more difficult music. Second, the consumer also must learn to play an instrument or sing for the music to be of any value. Consequently, sheet music has a symbiotic relationship with the rest of the industry. It fosters the further use of instruments and helps drive sales as musicians become more advanced. Conversely, for musicians there is a constant thirst for new music as they learn more musical skills.

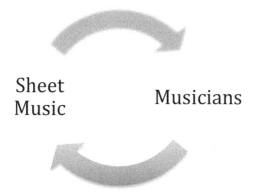

to become educated with the notation and open the gateway to

Because sheet music requires a consumer to be able to read music for it to be of value, sheet music is often one of the first products added as a supplemental sale beyond educational lessons. Often, music teachers will purchase the required learning materials from a music vendor and later resell these to students, either as a separate sale or included in the lesson fees charged to the consumer. Consequently, educators become significant "influencers" in the marketplace and are a target for marketing by the publishers. Workshops, reading sessions, and the like are often coordinated with local dealers to educate teachers on new teaching materials and other publications.

In addition to traditional sheet music notation, tablature has become a popular entry point for new musicians playing guitar. This hybrid form of music uses a different form of notation to demonstrate the finger pedagogy for guitar. In essence, tablature is a form of transcription of a particular artist playing a musical work. There is some debate between musicians as to whether tablature aids as an entry point into reading traditional notation, or acts as a hindrance. But, regardless, tablature has helped many beginning students take an active interest in learning the guitar and assisted in the growth of that market.

The forms and styles of sheet music are as varied as the individuals that play it. For most musicians, it acts as an ongoing, insatiable appetite for new material. For music stores that choose to carry it, print music acts as a draw for musicians to revisit their local store to see what is new. And, like much of our consumer world, musicians are turning to print music Internet sites to shop, as well. Large **"paper houses"** such as J.W. Pepper have become an invaluable resource for consumers. Technology shifts have allowed consumers to view PDF files of music online and links to recordings of the music works to preview before purchasing. Many of the print publishers have similar sites that organize their catalog, show previews or recordings, and in some cases allow for purchases directly from their site.

Product Lines

Sheet music comes in many different forms and different publishers often specialize in specific market niches. Other publishers are much larger and represent a wide range of music. Like the indie record industry, it is not uncommon for small, independent writers to self publish with the hopes of someday being purchased or consolidated into a major publisher with a larger distribution base. Major publishers like Hal Leonard and Alfred have a long history of purchasing the distribution rights of smaller, niche publishers or acting as the U.S. distributor for foreign publishers.

It is also important to understand the difference between a traditional **"publisher"** and a **"print publisher"**. When a songwriter creates a musical work and a copyright is established, the writer will often choose to enter into an agreement with a publisher to assist with the marketing and monetization of the music. The bundle of copyrights granted to the writer can be sold or transferred to a publisher. The publisher then tries to market the music to a record label for an artist to record or license it to a music supervisor for use in various media such as jingles, movies, tv, etc. Most of these publishers are not in the business of printing sheet music from these songs, as they are not actually in the printing business.

If a title is relatively successful, a publisher may wish to also sell it in print form. To do so, the traditional publisher will often transfer the print rights to a "print publisher" to create the actual sheet music. These print rights often have a shorter lifespan than the relationship between the composer and the traditional publisher. If the print contract expires without being renewed, the print rights revert back to the copyright holder. This is why you may see titles become "permanently out of print" with a particular print publisher.

Print publishers that specialize in educational or sacred music may secure the print licenses directly from the writers without involving an intermediary traditional publisher. It is common for these print publishers to develop exclusive relationships with particular writers to develop their catalog. Because this music often falls outside of the pop market, the sole purpose of their writing is for print publishing. Conversely, it is not uncommon for print publishing staff writers to arrange the more successful pop tunes for other derivative uses. This is especially common if the print publisher is owned or exclusively contracted by the more mainstream traditional publisher.

Print publishers divide their product lines into a variety of large categories and often have sub-categories within those. As we will see later when discussing new issue stocking programs, these categories allow the end retailer to customize the mix of music to reflect their specific markets. A general list is shown on the next page.

Print Music Categories

- Piano Methods
- Piano Supplemental Materials (Classical folios, Individual sheets, etc.)
- Piano/Vocal/Guitar Folios
- Band & Orchestral Instrument Methods
- Concert Band, Jazz, & Orchestral Arrangements
- Instrumental Solos & Ensembles
- Choral Arrangements
- Vocal Methods and Collections
- Elementary Classroom Methods and Musicals
- Guitar Methods
- Guitar Music and Tablature
- Handbell Music
- Supplemental Aids and Resources (Music dictionaries, textbooks, etc.)

Sales & Marketing Strategies

It has been said that carrying print music is a "Space-eating, Cash-consuming Monster!" And, without proper management, fiscal oversights, and inventory controls, it can be just that. However, it can also be a source of profit and a great marketing tool that drives customers into a retail music store to browse for new music and shop for everything else a store might carry. For survival, a retailer must constantly re-invent new ideas to encourage traffic to the store, and repeatedly purchased items such as music and accessories do just that. So, while print music may or may not be a cash cow for a business, it serves an equally important role as an important marketing tool for the store.

To remain viable, the store needs to turn its inventory periodically to reflect newer titles, while still keeping essential resources such as method books always on hand. For the publishers, it is also critical to get the new music they have created into the stores and in front of potential customers. However, there is a shelf life for a lot of music, especially pop titles that are hot one day and yesterday's news tomorrow. One of the biggest challenges for retailers is to balance music inventory that will turn quickly and represents new titles, without being stuck with unmoving, old inventory that ties up cash. Due in part to the easy ability for consumers to photocopy, sheet music is generally not returnable to the publisher once it is purchased by the retailer. This risk factor creates an obstacle for publishers wishing to make sure their new music is represented. Consequently, many publishers have come up with a "**New Issue Program**" for their dealers, which transfers some of the risk back to the publisher, but at a cost.

New Issues
Many print music publishers have "New Issue Programs" to which dealers can subscribe. Essentially, a subscribing dealer is automatically sent a few copies of any new music that the publisher has released. The dealer must accept the merchandise and pay for it whenever it is sent, usually in small batches across the whole fiscal year. In turn, the dealer is granted more aggressive discounts on daily orders placed throughout the year. With larger publishers that represent many different categories of music, dealers can specify particular categories of new issues releases. This allows the dealers the ability to tailor their inventory to reflect their local market. However, only categories in which they have subscribed will be allowed the steeper discounts for subsequent daily orders. For example, a dealer who subscribes only to piano/vocal new issues will get the higher discount on special orders for other piano/vocal titles, but it would not receive the same high discount for piano method books. The advantage of new issue programs to the publisher is that their music catalog is fully represented by participating stores. New items are more likely to be sold if they are in stock and retailers are sometimes hesitant to take on new items without a proven track

record of sales. The advantage to retailers is that it guarantees fresh merchandise. They receive more aggressive discounts on daily orders, which can be quite important in an industry that often has small margins. This is especially true with smaller publishers. The risk to dealers is that they have virtually no input as to what is being sent to them or when, and yet they must pay for all of it. While some of the merchandise will clearly sell, some will not. Dealers must use careful oversight to make sure they are selling through in each of the categories to which they have subscribed, and determine if the added discount on daily orders supersedes the additional cost of the extra merchandise.

Stocking Programs

Another way for publishers to enhance their representation in retail outlets without shifting the inventory risk to the dealers is through publisher **stocking programs**. Essentially, subscribing dealers agree to stock an entire section of this year's publications but are granted some return ability options. Unlike new issues where only one or two copies of a piece are sent with no return ability, stocking programs ship significant quantities of the new pieces. The music is returnable up to a specified date, either in its entirety or a limited percentage. The percentage is usually tied to the total dollar amount and not to a specific title. This allows a retailer to return the entire lot of a poor seller and perhaps none of something that has sold through.

Clinic Support

Another strategy used by publishers to enhance sales is to provide clinic support at the retail level. Publishers sponsor their contracted staff writers to visit retail stores and host clinics on new music or methods. When doing so, music is often advanced to the store to be given out as demo copies or sold at a special discounted price to attendees. Usually, the publisher will ask that "back-up stock" of the featured music is also purchased by the store. All or a percentage of this stock may be returnable within a particular time frame to shift the inventory risk away from the retailer.

A similar program is used for reading sessions. Reading sessions are sponsored by retailers to showcase new music. Music educators, choir directors, and the like come together to sing or rehearse new music. This helps them select music they might use in upcoming concerts, church services, etc. Clinic packets are assembled by the retailer to be given as free samples to the directors. Music is sent by the publishers at "**print cost**", basically pennies per copy, and the corners of the copies are chopped to indicate they are not for resale. To qualify for print cost, most publishers will ask for an additional order of "back-up stock" which may or may not be guaranteed returnable within a specified time.

Supplier-Dealer Chain

For decades, the print music market has been dependent on merchandising its products alongside traditional musical instruments and accessories in retail music stores. While we have seen a shift to some online sales for digital downloading of sheet music, the biggest shift has been more of a hybrid. Large "**paper houses**" (stores that only sell sheet music) now have very sophisticated web sites that allow consumers the ability to preview some or all of the music and often times provide a listening track. Consumers can make their selections and the professionally bound paper copies of the music are then sent to the customer via a ground delivery system.

Despite this, the traditional **brick and mortar** business model is the bread and butter of the industry. It allows print music to be married with other musical purchases and is the best way to connect with the publishers' target market. Due to the sheer volume of written music, customers often need the assistance of trained sheet music sales professionals to find the music editions they seek. Often, the consumer may have limited knowledge of music, especially in early stages of learning, and the task of finding something both suitable and playable can be daunting.

However, publishers certainly are aware of the move towards a more digital marketplace. In some cases, publishers have allowed consumers to purchase directly from the publisher's website. To avoid disrupting the time-honored retail relationships the publishers have established with their dealer network, there are usually two approaches used to include the retailer. One is to simply kick back a percentage of the sales that are done directly with the publisher to the local dealer in the consumer's market. Another is to actually mask the publisher's web portal within the dealer's. In other words, while it looks like you are purchasing from the retailer directly, you are in fact accessing the database of the publisher and the music is sent out directly from them and the music is charged to the dealer's account. This rather cumbersome approach has been tried by various publishers, but a more practical approach has been to do this with just digital downloads. In this scenario, the consumer discovers the music on the retailer's website, purchases a digital download, prints it at home or in the store, and the publisher charges a fee directly to the retailer for access to their digital catalog.

So, while the digital hybrid seems to work well with single copies of tunes, folios (collections of tunes) are often left to the more traditional sales approach within the brick and mortar environment. This allows the consumer to still have a professionally bound book. To this end, it seems that the marketing of traditional printed music will continue as it has, but will continue to incorporate technological efficiencies where possible.

Financing

Unlike its instrument or accessory counterparts, the margins on sheet music are relatively small. While it is possible to find 50% discount terms with some of the larger publishers if retailers are subscribing to new issue programs, it is not uncommon for the discounts to be more in the 30-40% range. Coupled with this is the fact that handling sheet music has some built in complexities that drive up the internal costs of handling the product. Consequently, while some retailers may discount music 10-15% off of list, it is not uncommon for the music to be sold at full sticker price. Sheet music is often an add-on sale or even an impulse buy for consumers, and the music itself is not generally terribly expensive. As a result, sheet music is much less price sensitive than other musical items, such as instruments. This resistance by retailers to significantly discount this product also means that publishers do not establish any type of Minimum Advertised Prices.

The internal costs for retailers are substantial. Handling sheet music takes a well-trained staff that can adequately research titles. Even this task can be daunting as "titles" for music are not copyrighted. This means that many pieces of music can be called the same thing, creating a great deal of confusion in the market. It would not be the first time for a consumer to order a Christian pop title for a wedding only to be surprised with a heavy metal thrash song!

The sheer volume of available sheet music creates its own costs. A retailer can choose which brands of guitar strings or keyboards it carries. But if a customer wants a particular song, it is pretty hard to substitute it for something else. This forces retailers to carry music with dozens and dozens of publishers, each with their own stocking policies, discounts, new issue programs, etc. It is very easy for a retailer to let their inventories balloon out of control. Also, most pop music can become stale very quickly. What was yesterday's blockbuster hits, are today's leftovers. All the discounting in the world won't move some of these titles once they have gone cold.

Publisher discounts to music retailers vary but are usually tied into both volume and new issue programs. As discussed earlier, retailers that subscribe to new issue programs are sent new music in the categories to which they have subscribed. Any additional orders in these categories will come at a larger discount than the standard rate. The other way that retailers can increase their discounts on music is through stock orders.

Stock orders are large orders placed once or twice a year with the publisher to "restock" the retailer with familiar staples. Method books, vocal collections, manuscript paper, decade books, and so forth are ordered in volume. The retailer must keep robust records of which common titles "turn" easily and are "must-haves" for the store. Usually, the publisher offers an additional 5% or so off of the normal maximum discounts for the relative categories. Additionally, longer repayment terms are often offered. Standard terms for sheet music publishers are 30 days. Stock order programs may offer repayment terms of 60 or 90 days.

Pricing Structure

As mentioned previously, sheet music tends to be sold at or near its list price. The relatively low list price of most music coupled by its high cost of inventory, demands that retailers keep their margins as high as possible. The high cost of shipping is another factor that drives up the overall cost to the music; paper is simply heavy when shipped in quantity. When higher discounting is done by stores, it is often used as a "loss leader" to drive the sales of other merchandise.

It should also be noted that copyright forces the retailer to only purchase the music titles from the specific publisher that owns the copyrights. While a few wholesalers handle music, most stores with any kind of substantial sheet music department form alliances directly with the publishers. This proprietary aspect of music means that a publisher has strong control over the pricing of its titles. This is substantially different than say, the accessory market, where products are often sold through many different distribution channels.

While the copyright provides a strong protection from fraud while they have the distribution rights, it can also present a challenge. This is especially true when publishing folios, or collections of tunes. If even one tune's copyright contract with the print publisher expires and is not renewed, the entire book can no longer be sold. There is usually a six month window to allow sell-through of existing stock, but once that expires the books must be destroyed. This is why consumers will often find something is "out of print". A title that is "temporarily out of print" is usually an indication that the music is out of stock at the warehouse and must be reprinted. But, a title that is "permanently out of stock" is usually an indication that the print distribution rights were not renewed by the publisher. That is, they lost copyright. Publishers sometimes combat this problem with folios by substituting the lost title with one they do own. This is why a folio may be republished as a "revised edition."

Future

What was once a pretty stale, unchanging business model has seen a great deal of changes driven mostly by technology. Sheet music scored and read directly from a computer tablet for example could replace more traditional paper copies. However, with technology also comes a loss of control. You need look no further than the record industry to see that digital formats make piracy and quick illegal replication hard to control.

The Music Products Industry

Regardless, there will always be a form of sheet music merchandising. Exactly what form that takes remains to be seen. But, as long as there are musicians, there will be an insatiable need for music and the ones that compose and sell it!

Chapter 7

The Commercial Audio Market

The Marketplace

Imagine being in a ball park in 1920. The smack of the bat, the roar of the crowd, and the static crackle of an announcer from a primitive horn on a wooden pole is as American as hotdogs and apple pie. You can almost imagine Babe Ruth tipping his hat to the cheering fans. While this Utopian world was acceptable at the turn of the last century, today's ball parks, sports arenas, and other large gathering spaces have turned into more than just neighborhood novelties. They are giant, sophisticated, multi-purpose facilities that host concerts, theatrical events, church services, political rallies, and all kinds of spectacles that blend not only audio, but visual and graphic elements. The audience is submersed into the entire experience!

There have been transformative events in history that have changed the music industry. With the advent of the rock 'n roll era, fans demanded to see their favorite entertainers in live concert settings. Artists like Elvis Presley and Def Leppard had troves of fans that would not fit into a traditional theater setting. Their giant fanbase demanded larger venues, and concert promoters often turned to sports arenas and civic auditoriums to handle the crowds. The advent of this wildly popular music would not only turn the music industry upside down, it would transform the way in which the public experienced these shows. No longer could the artist be dependent on a primitive public address system used for announcing ball games. A new, modern approach to audio reinforcement was demanded and the commercial audio market was born.

Performing artists were beginning to push the envelope. When playing bigger venues they did not want to be performing through an underpowered and poorly adapted house public address system. Early bands did not even want to be heard live on T.V. because the playback and recording systems in early studios were sub-par and did not represent the new sound quality being represented in newly released LPs.

It was the perfect time in history for a transformation. Popular music was gaining traction driven by a quickly growing recording industry. New advances in technology, made possible by military hardware and space exploration funding, were being pushed down into consumer applications. And, the solid state transistor and other related technologies were making once impossible applications both easy and cheap.

While not directly in the music business, Bell Labs were at the forefront to much of this change as they looked to consumer applications for their new scientific advancements. Spearheading this movement was Harry F. Olsen, a Bell Labs engineer that pioneered these advancements and to this day is considered to be the father of modern audio engineering.

In 1966, Roy and Gene Clair began their historic career in audio reinforcement when they created a sound system to amplify Frankie Valli and the Four Seasons in concert. They soon became pioneers of the live concert venue. Much of their new concepts, including two way loud-speakers, slanted stage monitors, and eventually flown line array speaker cabinets, are considered standard stage protocol even today.

Other pioneers such as Jim Gamble of Tycobrahe Sound Systems would modernize the portable and tour-rugged mixing console allowing live sound to easily tour with performing bands. Legendary artists such as Ian Anderson of Jethro Tull, The Beach Boys, and even Stevie Wonder quickly adopted their hardware and put it to use on the road. Additionally, Tychobrahe focused on creating separate monitor mixes so that artists could recreate on stage what was being heard in the larger venue.

It was becoming clear that the future of live production had moved out of the small concert theater and onto the big stage. The challenge to provide consistent and professional live sound as these venues grew created an entirely new segment of the industry. Other major players such as Showco, which would later be purchased by Clair Brothers, focused on this growing need to fill large arenas and amphitheaters with proper live sound, whether on a permanent basis or a portable tour. Companies like JBL and Crown would push the envelope with innovations to speakers and amplifiers to keep up with the growing market. The live commercial audio market would move from its infancy to its modern look today.

Customer Demographics

While the ultimate beneficiaries of the commercial audio products industry are technically the artists, they are often not directly in the sales process. Once an artist's gear crosses over from simple PA rigs used in local gigs to the commercial audio systems used to support large concert venues, these quickly become unaffordable to the performing artists. That being said, touring artists will often have specific audio requirements detailed in agency riders for live performances. These requirements must be met by either the promoter or the venue hosting the event to be in compliance with the artist's touring needs.

The Music Products Industry

As such, the two primary customers for commercial audio fall into two categories. First, performance venues purchase commercial sound systems to be used for repeated events. Whether it be a large sports arena, civic auditorium, or a large house of worship, a permanently installed commercial audio system engineered for the specific venue is built to suit the general purpose of the space. Acousticians work with architectural engineers to design a system for maximum versatility and a premium auditory experience.

The second customer for commercial audio equipment is the **"rental and staging"** market. Designed to provide portable systems that can either tour with contracted artists or provide temporary systems at local venues, rental companies purchase full systems that can be delivered temporarily for specific events. There are two basic rental options exercised by such companies. A **"dry hire"** rental involves simply leasing the rental equipment out to the user with no further operational support. Contrasting, a **"wet hire"** rental not only leases the equipment, but a supporting tech crew is supplied to operate the equipment.

Product Lines

The commercial audio market has dramatically changed from its early days. Today, the focus is on the convergence of not only basic audio, but lighting, video, computer graphics, and general information technology (IT). In fact, the least profitable part of the industry is really the audio side. Integrating all of the available technologies together into one package represents the growth in the industry. By doing so, the market becomes nearly limitless as every presentation conference room in a hotel, church, or corporate office is a potential market for integrated technologies.

As such, the product lines available for full line commercial audio dealers now encompass many different types of gear. Of course, the traditional components of the commercial audio industry would include the audio rigs. These include speaker line arrays, large power amplifiers, monitor systems, mixing consoles, and effects processing. Beyond the audio gear, other components began to integrate into the full show.

Probably first to be integrated were lighting systems that frequently accompany live shows. As these are often rigged on some of the same hardware points as the commercial sound, it made sense to include lighting and similar effects as part of the performance package. Today, those effects can include fog machines, laser lights, and even pyrotechnics.

More recently, video components such as video walls, graphic effects, and the like are all part of the show. However, commercial audio dealers use similar integrated technologies to combine video, conferencing, audio, and lighting in all sorts of venues. This can be large civic auditoriums or simple small conference rooms. The commercial audio provider has now become an AV Integrator of many diverse technologies.

When the technology is permanently installed for the end user, there needs to be a careful balance between supplying an integrated interface for all of these technologies and one that is still user friendly. As more and more technologies are added this becomes an ongoing challenge. Supplying technical support is now as much a part of the entire product as the gear itself. The national average for such support can range from $85-125 per hour and can be provided either on or off site.

Sales & Marketing Strategies

As civic auditoriums and other large spaces are constructed or renovated, integrated commercial systems are often let out for bid. For permanently installed commercial systems retail suppliers often act as general contractors for these projects. For large undertakings, a senior project manager may be provided to the venue as part of the bid to oversee the entire install.

Unlike the Pro Audio Combo market, MAP pricing is not often very relevant except perhaps on very high demand new technologies. Pricing is done as part of a package bid which may include many variables including installation, support, integration, and other services. Inventory is kept at a minimum and only brought in on a **"just in time"** basis to satisfy the needs of the installation. A small inventory of accessories such as connectors, cables, and other similar parts are kept on hand for ease of use and to handle service work. There is no need to inventory the larger equipment as that will vary greatly from project to project and would only tie up cash for the retailer.

Inventory for the rental and staging retailers is significantly different. Since providing available gear is the very essence of their business model, keeping heavy amounts of inventory on hand is critical. The key, however, is making sure that inventory is in use at the consumer level as much as possible. It does no good to have inventory sitting in a warehouse and not out on lease. Whether it is a wet hire or dry hire, keeping cash flow coming in from this inventory is the only way a rental retailer can maintain such capital equipment demands.

For the rental market, inventory is divided into two fundamental categories. The first type of inventory is perishable goods. These are generally lower cost items that will wear out relatively quickly after only a few rental turns. Microphones, cables, lighting gels, and other smaller goods are considered perishable and are rented at a higher rate relative to their cost. Generally, a per use rental rate on these items reflect 8-15% of their actual cost. So, the retailer will recoup its investment on these in as little as 7 to 12 rental turns. This is necessary due to the higher wear rate on these items that will need to be replaced more frequently.

The second type of inventory is capital goods. These are generally higher priced items that have significantly longer shelf life and can be used many times before being replaced. Due to their higher cost, servicing damaged goods is more financially feasible and allows for extended life of the capital goods. Rental rates for capital items tend to range closer to 5% and thus take at least 20 rentals to recapture cost. The key with these items, however, is the after market. Beyond a 5 to 7 year amortization, these capital products can be resold as used goods in the open market to add to the retailer's ultimate bottom line and provide working capital to purchase new inventory. As it is often said in the rental market, "You just don't want to be the last person owning the gear!"

Supplier-Dealer Chain

Not unlike other product segments in the music industry, franchises for specific brands are negotiated between the retailer and the manufacturer. Typically, to carry a particular line of goods, a commercial audio retailer must be approved for a dealership. Minimum qualifications include having a base inventory to demonstrate products, keeping test equipment available to diagnose problems, and participating in ongoing training by the manufacturer to provide appropriate service minimums.

Generally, there is no initial inventory master order or "buy-in" imposed by the manufacturers. However, there is an expected level of yearly sales to keep a business account open and decent terms with the vendor. If sales slip below this minimum, the retailer runs the risk of having another competing business opened up in that territory or perhaps lose the franchise entirely.

While territories were once defined by specific geographic perimeters, today's e-commerce environment demands a much looser interpretation. Essentially, the factory sales manager and district sales rep for a franchised brand will determine market penetration based on sales history and density of the market. There is a need for a careful balance between adequate representation of the brand in a region and creating an environment where a retailer can operate profitably by being loyal to the brand.

Margins in the commercial audio and integrated AV markets have been falling in recent years. While as little as five years ago a 36% margin was the industry standard, that has now been trimmed to as little as 20%. Anything below this effectively become unsustainable by the commercial audio retailer. Adequate margins need to be built into ever project to recover from inevitable, unforeseen problems. Even a simple issue involving a warranted defective piece of equipment can become a nightmare for a service retailer after it is permanently installed. Liability for such problems can become a bargaining tool for a retailer when negotiating margins.

Financing

Commercial audio products can be quite expensive to inventory. While the rental and staging businesses must carry a significant debt load of inventory to be operational, the permanent installer and AV integrator can purchase inventory as the installation projects are approved.

Financing terms from manufacturers can vary according to the products and the business relationships established between the vendor and the retailer. While the industry standard of 30 days net still applies to much of the market, longer terms can be negotiated. Clearly, due to the significant cost of these products, cash flow can be a huge concern.

To address this, initial down-payments must be made before work can begin and "progress payments" are often required at specific intervals to fund the next phase of the work. This allows the retailer access to cash when inventory needs to be purchased and keeps the entire project properly capitalized without risk of work interruptions.

Other financing options for commercial audio retailers can include third party lending sources that provide capital where traditional banking options might not. Financial outlets such as Lighthouse Financial Corporation have traditionally provided funding in this market segment for growing businesses. Also, DK Capital has both true leasing and capital leasing options for retailers, especially those in the rental and staging market.

Manufacturers of very high end gear may also require the products to be purchased by the audio retailer through an authorized distributor. This designated distributor receives the product from the manufacturer and resells it to the retailer. While this gives up some of the margin that the manufacturer would earn from the sale, it shifts the burden of having to warehouse and fund the inventory to the distributor. Likewise the responsibility of collecting on payables from the retailer is alleviated from the manufacturer and pushed down to the more localized distributor level.

Pricing Structure

As mentioned above, MAP pricing is rarely an issue in the commercial audio market as there are numerous variables to the installation field, and the rental and staging market is only involved in selling used, depreciated merchandise. The exception to this is in the lower end "consumable" merchandise market that may be supported by either a manufacturer or a distributor model. In many cases, this distributor model is used to fill orders for smaller dealers that either cannot sell enough product to support a dealership or have a need for a product they rarely sell. However, the products are limited to the lower end consumable market and would have limited access to higher ticket, franchised merchandise.

This side of the business begins to cross over into the Pro Audio Combo market discussed earlier. These two markets share some of the same products but vary in virtue of sheer scale and type of end user. It is also why the commercial audio market is only partly represented at trade shows such as NAMM, but is best represented at InfoComm International. This trade organization represents audiovisual and communication integrators. There are numerous other trade organizations that can also be involved due to the crossover nature of this ever-expanding business. The most notable include Integrated Systems Europe (ISE) and Pro Lighting & Sound Association (PLASA) for European vendors and the U.S. Institute for Theatre Technology (USITT) for retailers serving the theatrical stage market.

Pricing models within this market segment can vary. But in light of today's highly competitive and transparent environment, any serious vendor in the integration business is being billed at "**end column**". That is, the retailer is paying the lowest possible price offered regardless of quantity purchased. While there may be occasional price breaks for case quantities on certain items, these are more likely to occur with consumables that cross over to traditional MI dealers.

There may, however, be price incentives for contracted integrators to substitute brands within the specifications of a bid. Further discounts can be earned if the integrator is also the designer for the installation project, as this retailer is in the position to recommend or demand specific models and brands. These discounts can be as high as 15%. Further discounts for "quick pay" receipts are standard for the music products industry and range from 2-3% for payments within 21 days of receipt of goods.

Future

While traditionally developed through the entertainment business as commercial audio, today this market segment has truly become the commercial integrated technology business and has crossed over into many different industries. No longer does it simply consist of a front of the house engineer running audio for a band. In fact, the live entertainment side of the industry now represents only a small portion of the market.

It was once said that the live concerts are like Vegas slot machines, Broadway theater productions are like blackjack tables, but the movies are the back room poker games. To make a lot of money one needs to go where a lot of money changes hands. For the commercial audio business that future resides in the large video/audio integration projects that combine multiple technologies into a future that is nearly incomprehensible. That is where the action is and where the big money trades hands.

To be successful today, and audio engineer needs to be on the cutting edge of all of these technologies and understand how each can be integrated into the other. For live sound, house audio can be mixed on a handheld tablet, divorced of the myriad of snakes and wires. A performer can dial an in-ear monitor mix from his smart phone without even the intervention of an engineer. The use of a civic space can be transformed from a concert hall to a conference center just from the pallet of integrated technologies at the hand of the engineer.

Perhaps no segment of the music products industry shows more potential for growth and change like that of the integrated commercial audio business. Imagination is the only limit to its success!

The Music Products Industry

Chapter 8

The Accessory Market

The Marketplace

While most people are familiar with all of the cool instruments and music gear found in a music store that drives the music products industry, the bulk of the day to day transactions are often found on a much smaller scale. The accessory market is one of the most viable and important segments in the music industry. This is because it continuously drives customers back into the market to pick up the needed supplies to make music. A car salesperson may only sell a car to someone every few years, but the gas stations sell fuel to that customer every week. Similarly, a consumer may only be able to purchase a new instrument occasionally, but he will be back time and time again to buy new strings, reeds, cables, and all of the other smaller items that make it possible to continue to play.

The accessory market it made up of smalls, but collectively they add up to a huge portion of the market. And, by constantly supplying the musician with these necessary items, the store and sales staff are able to maintain a relationship with the customer between bigger sales. Most accessory sales are under $100 and many are under $20, but the margins can often be better than slaying the elephant in the highly competitive instrument market. Besides acting as repeat purchases between these larger transactions, they can also serve as lucrative add-ons at the time of the larger sales.

Even in down economies, accessories often shine as a bright spot. This is sometimes known as the "lipstick effect". Historically, in times of economic weakness the sale of lipstick shows a significant uptick. This can be attributed to the fact that while a consumer might not spring for an expensive purchase such as a new evening gown, they will buy something small that is new and makes them feel good. Similarly, a musician might not be able to buy a brand new guitar at this time, but he can buy new strings, a tuner, or an effects pedal to keep an interest in his hobby.

Regardless of good times or bad, accessories are a profitable component of every music store. It is an easy way for a retailer to freshen its inventory without a huge financial commitment. New SKUs can be added or subtracted to keep things interesting for the customer and provide ample new products for salespeople to demonstrate and suggest.

Customer Demographics

The overall market for accessory sales really has no boundaries. Traditionally, the market would certainly be existing musicians having to purchase products that wear out. These "consumables", as they are called, are any items that are used to make an instrument work properly and wear out with use. These include items such as guitar strings, valve oil, woodwind reeds, drum sticks, and thousands of other replacement items. Purchases of these consumables are directly related to the frequency of their use with instruments.

Additionally, music accessories may be purchased as add-on items to increase the functionality of an instrument. These tend to be pricier items such as guitar pedals, tuners, cases, microphones, and the like. Because the margins on these items tend to be greater than their related instruments, these accessories can be a healthy profit source for both the store and the salesperson.

While we tend to think of musicians as being the primary consumer for music accessories, often these items can be a gateway into creating new musicians. Simple accessories such harmonicas, melodicas, or even inexpensive ukuleles can spark an interest in pursuing music at a higher level. Grade school students are often taught basic music skills on recorders in general music classes as a way to introduce reading music and get them excited about possibly taking up a band instrument in the future.

Product Lines

Music accessories are manufactured by thousands of vendors from all over the world. Some are made by large music product manufacturers, others by tiny vendors literally made in someone's basement. Distribution for these products vary widely, due in part to who actually manufactures the goods. Music accessories fall into two categories; proprietary and nonproprietary goods. Proprietary goods are those that are made and distributed exclusively by the manufacturer. While in some cases the actual production of these products might be outsourced to a separate factory, the products are branded exclusively to the manufacturer. For example, a retailer can stock Yamaha Valve Oil, which is sold directly by Yamaha to the retailer. However, Yamaha also carries Rico brand clarinet reeds as part of their accessory division. The reeds are non-proprietary as they are not made by Yamaha. We will see that this can often become an issue when differentiating dealer discounts for accessory orders.

Sales & Marketing Strategies

Creating brand loyalty to specific musical accessories is always in the interest of the manufacturer. To create this there is some limited use of endorsing artists. While we have seen that instrument manufacturers generally do not just give away instrument to endorsing artists, accessory manufacturers may be much more generous. It is common for manufacturers to send sample products to artists to encourage use. Likewise, retailers are often sent samples of new products, hoping to have their SKUs added to the store's inventory.

While some accessory products have strong margins, others tend to be much more competitive. The difference comes from a product's adoption as a staple commodity in the market. Commodities are products that are purchased so frequently that they require virtually no sales interaction on the part of the retailer. As such, downward pricing pressure increases as the consumer is frequently in the market. Online retailers often capitalize on this by offering these items as loss leaders to attract consumers to their sites with hope of adding on more profitable products.

In response to this some manufacturers have established Minimum Advertising Policies (MAP) on products to both help the brick and mortar stores and to keep their products from being viewed as inferior. MAP pricing is especially sensitive for more expensive products such as cymbals or microphones. As discussed earlier, this tug of war for MAP pricing is an ongoing battle to help balance the playing field.

For non-commodity products, the accessory market is less price sensitive. It is not uncommon for a consumer to haggle over the price of a new instrument only to pay full retail for an add-on accessory such as a case or strap. In the end it is often the skill of the salesperson to market these extra items. Also, for many products brand loyalty is far less developed than it is for the related musical instrument. Stores will commonly create "house brand" accessories by purchasing in bulk and, in some cases, stencil the store's name or logo on the product. It is an avenue to create store identity on items that have little brand imprint on the larger market.

Supplier-Dealer Chain

The musical accessory market is a bit like the wild west. Franchise agreements are rare and are usually only found on higher end items. Generally speaking most retailers are able to get just about any accessory item that they desire provided they can support the inventory. There are two main sources for these products: manufacturers and wholesalers.

Depending on the manufacturer, proprietary goods distribution may only be allowed through authorized instrument dealers or these small goods might be released for distribution through a wholesale network. It just depends on how tightly the instrument maker wishes to control their brand. More often, however, they will release distribution of their instrument-branded accessories at least to a wholesaler, which can allow non-franchised stores to carry their small goods.

Larger accessory manufacturers that are not also instrument makers generally develop direct sales distribution relationships with the retailers. While occasionally franchised, usually the dealer agreements address issues such as pricing rather than limiting distribution. The accessory market is all about volume, not exclusivity, since the overall price of the goods are usually small.

Smaller accessory makers rely heavily on music wholesalers to distribute their products. Wholesale distributors usually represent huge numbers of SKUs from many manufacturers. Generally, they operate on fairly thin margins but move large quantities of goods. Industry dominant wholesalers include

The Music Products Industry

Harris Teller, KMC Music, St. Louis Music, Musicorp, and many others.

Wholesalers perform two very important roles in the music industry. First, they allow smaller manufacturers access to a pre-established distribution system in the industry. This shifts the credit and collection responsibilities to the wholesaler's pre-established dealer network. In other words, the manufacturer only must sell to a handful of wholesalers instead of an unlimited number of retailers. Second, retailers can turn to a single source to find many obscure music products. They can use their pre-established credit lines with the wholesaler, instead of constantly opening up new vendor accounts. It is a win-win for both sides of the equation, and the wholesaler takes a small cut to be the middleman.

Financing

Depending on the source of the accessory products, financing can take on different forms. Wholesale distributors rarely extend any dating past 30 days, if that. For smaller, less-established retailers, payments may need to be COD or prepaid on a company credit card. Because of the thin margins and the wide expanse of dealers in their network, they are rarely in a position to offer any significant dating on these small goods.

For larger accessory manufacturers selling directly to retailers 30 day dating terms are standard. However, instrument manufacturers will often include an accessory component to the franchise requirements for their instrument lines. Financing on master orders which include accessory items can have dating terms of a couple of months or the opportunity to include free freight.

Pricing Structure

Because small goods such as music accessories are often purchased in bulk quantities, net pricing is often connected to the size of the order. Quantity discounts usually apply and in some cases, fees are charged for odd-lot orders or broken case quantities.

One common pricing technique is known as order **accumulated earned discounts**. Rather than forcing the retailer to purchase a large master order to achieve a specific discount level, the retailer's combined purchases through the year count toward discount plateaus. Once achieving that plateau, every subsequent order receives an extra earned discount. So, for example, the first $1000 net in orders might qualify for a 50% net. Once this is achieved, every order after that might receive an additional 5%. These discount structures can either reset at the end of the fiscal year, or continue provided that the retailer purchase at least the same amount the subsequent year.

Please note that the extra 5% is applied to the already discounted 50%, not to the MSRP. In other words, the extra 5% does <u>not</u> translate to a 55% discount.

Example:
    (50%+5%)
    $100 MSRP X 50% = $50 X 5% = $2.50
    $50 - $2.50 = $47.50
vs.
    (55%)
    $100 MSRP X 55% = $55
    $100 - $55.00 = $45.00

Other companies require a yearly master order that will set the discount for all subsequent orders for the year. Rather than the accumulation technique described above, these require one large order. Usually the size of that order will have various breakpoints at which a larger discount will apply. There may also be some requirements that are tied to the number of proprietary SKUs rather than a set dollar amount. This is to encourage the dealer to represent a broad array of the manufacturer's products rather than just loading up on a few good sellers. Often, by doing this a retailer may discover new products that sell better than expected.

Finally, a manufacturer may use freight incentives to increase the volume of the order. This can be done in two ways. One is to ship the order freight-free if it meets a certain dollar minimum. This encourages retailers to forecast sales and order in bulk from the manufacturer, minimizing transactions and the associated processing expenses.

A second method is to apply a **freight allowance**. This has become more popular as the cost of freight has increased with the rise in fuel prices. This process applies a discount to the freight charge as a percentage of the net price of the order. It is possible for the retailer to obtain free freight, but the net cost of the order must exceed the expense of the freight. Often to obtain this, a savvy retailer will add some high dollar, but light-weight items to an order that has heavier goods. This increases the overall net without substantially increasing the weight of the shipment and the subsequently higher freight charges.

Future

For most music retailers, accessory sales add a lot of value to their store. These higher margin items contribute substantially to the bottom line. The constant mix of goods keeps the store's inventory looking fresh. The constant need for ancillary items keep customers returning to the store. Because of all of this, the accessory market will remain healthy for years to come and tends to remain more resistant to economic swings in the market. There is a certain entrepreneurial spirit to this segment of the industry as everyone tries to re-invent a better musical mousetrap. As such, the musical accessory market will always remain a solid component to the music products industry.

The Music Products Industry

Chapter 9

The Service and Repair Market

The Marketplace

While the vast majority of the music industry involves selling physical products, providing service and repair work to these products is another huge market. This can be done in one of two ways. The service can be done as a stand-alone independent business or it can be part of a service department within a retail store. Most music stores provide at least some type of service and repair department in order to establish customer loyalty and add value to products that might be found cheaper online.

In-house repair departments have several advantages to the retailer. New inventory can be set up correctly and prepped for sale. Guitars, for example, often have to have their necks adjusted for proper string height depending on the temperature and humidity of the location. Band instruments coming off of rental programs must be cleaned and regulated before being leased again. Pianos must be tuned after delivery both to the store and later to the purchaser. By keeping this process all in-house the store is able to provide fast service to the customer. Retailers are also able to quickly deal with problems that a customer might experience with a new product or an issue that comes up at the last minute before a performance. In-house departments allow the retailer to adjust the queue and prioritize the customer repairs accordingly.

Of course, this comes at a cost. Additional employees on the clock means that the service department is only profitable if they are busy, preferably with chargeable repairs. With some product segments, such as the school band market this can also be very seasonal, being overwhelmed in the summer and overstaffed in the spring. There is also a large investment in equipment and parts. Some extremely complex jobs, such as full overhauls, may require a business to own machinery that is only seldom used. In any case, investing in an in-house repair department can be an expensive but often necessary evil.

In addition to in-house service departments, some repair staff open their own independent businesses and deal both directly with consumers or indirectly by contracting work through a music store. These shops are often able to take on larger, more complex jobs, specializing in work that an average music store might not support. Of course, they have the same large (or larger) investment in parts and equipment that the store has without the benefit of having retail product sales help to support the service business.

Customer Demographics

As mentioned earlier, there are two general types of customers for service work. First, is the actual consumer who will need periodic service on instruments and gear that is being used. This can involve general maintenance such as lubrication, changing worn pads or strings, and general regulation. It can also involve fixing actual damage that has occurred, restoring the instrument back to its original condition. The second customer is the actual store itself, ensuring that their products are in good, working condition and repairing any damage done to used or rental items. It is easy for a store to undervalue the importance of this second customer. By keeping the products in perfect working order, the store is able to keep the money flowing and the consumers happy

Product Lines

There are five primary types of repair technicians, each specializing in a different area. Interestingly, there tends to be little crossover or doubling of these areas.

Band Instrument Repair Technician
These technicians work on brass and woodwind instruments, often specializing in a particular area or even instrument for larger stores. Smaller stores with fewer service techs often have to cover a range of instrument repairs. Technicians must be able to competently play all of the instruments in order to play test completed repairs.

Orchestral Luthier
These technicians work on orchestra instruments including violins, violas, celli, and basses. Woodworking skills are a must as it often requires rebuilding very fragile components of the instruments. Luthiers will also rehair and repair orchestra bows.

Guitar Technician/Luthier
These technicians work on both acoustic and electric guitars. Usually guitar players themselves, their work involves properly setting up necks and strings into regulation, filing frets, adjusting bridges and nuts, etc. Additionally, some basic electronics work is required to rewire plugs, pickups, and attenuator knobs. Guitar technicians commonly travel with major entertainment acts to keep the show's equipment in tip top shape.

Electronic Technician
Today it requires a junior electrical engineer to work on the massive amounts of electronic gear found in most music stores. These technicians must be skilled at diagnosing problems with keyboards, amplifiers, P.A. equipment, and microphones.

Piano Tuner/Technician

These technicians work both in and out of the store, often going to customers' homes to tune acoustic pianos. Some technicians have full restoration workshops, rebuilding old pianos and finding them new homes.

Sales & Marketing Strategies

In today's highly competitive market, service components of a business have become increasingly important for brick and mortar businesses. There needs to be a reason to shop locally and avoid the big box chains and the online commerce sites. Having a repair shop on site can be a very valuable marketing tool. Perhaps nowhere is this more important than for the school music dealer. As discussed earlier, this business model involves giving very expensive and intricate instruments to ten-year-olds to carry to and from school. This is just asking for trouble! Having a repair shop to keep the rental stock working properly can often mean the difference between having the student stay in the music program or not.

Frankly, some sort of minimal shop is imperative for any music store. Much like the auto business, most of the products in an average retail music store are test played before they are purchased. Keeping the products in working, salable condition falls to the service shop.

Supplier-Dealer Chain

While the most familiar use of repair services is that which is contained within a retail music store, similar kinds of services are also employed at the manufacturer level. Most products have some type of manufacturer warranty. Fixing problems with instruments or gear that is under warranty is usually handled in one of two ways.

The retailer can elect to fix the problem on site and bill the manufacturer. To do this usually requires prior approval from the vendor or some sort of pre-determined process and billing rate. Simple problems are often handled this way, if for no other reason, to expedite the repair for the customer. In fact, the vendor may prefer this for known defects or recalls. In these cases, certain retailers may become "certified warranty centers" and may even do warranty work for other retailers.

The second option is to ship the instrument back to the manufacturer for warranty work. Many manufacturers have the retailer do this not only to insure a proper repair behind which the vendor can stand, but also to try to determine what caused the problem. From this investigation manufacturers can make design changes or process adjustments to keep the issue from recurring in the future.

Having a source of proper parts can also be an issue for a store. Parts may only be available to actual franchised dealers. As a result, a store may have to limit their work to the specific brands they actually carry. One work-around in the school band business is Allied Supply, which acts as a parts wholesaler for many different manufacturers. However, lately the flood of new off-shore manufacturers have made parts availability much more challenging. Customers are often surprised to discover that what seemed like a great deal on a cheap product has now turned into a "disposable" instrument!

Financing

As we discussed in the chapter on the School Band market, maintenance and service work on band and orchestra instruments is often included as part of a monthly rental fee. If this fee is broken out separately as part of the monthly fee, as it often is, shop fees for rental customer work should be charged internally against that income source. This more accurately accounts for the "free work" that is being done for internal rental customers. Likewise, shop fees calculated for service plans or extended warranty work should be expensed against the service plan income generated by selling extended warranties.

Calculating the value of a service department can often be deceptively difficult. While it is possible to account for billable repair services and the related employee, equipment, and parts costs, they are only part of the equation. The added value that having on-site service brings to a store is often reflected in both higher margins and increased traffic. In many ways, even a service department that is only minimally breaking even can be considered a necessary evil and simply part of the cost of doing business.

Pricing Structure

Repair and service pricing is usually done on a time and materials basis. Often, a store will calculate the time that a standard service takes and create a preset price. Otherwise, many customers prefer to have a written or verbal estimate at the time the instrument is dropped off. Some stores may charge for this estimate, especially if there is disassembly involved to diagnose the problem. If work is authorized, sometimes this estimate charge may be applied towards the work being done.

Depending on the employment relationship of the technicians with the store, payroll can vary for the workers. Some stores allow the shop to function as a separate business unit within the store and the technicians are paid based on a commission on billed units. This can get complicated, however, when store stock inventory is serviced. Usually the rate paid to the technicians is reduced for store stock work.

Other stores simply hire the technicians as regular employees that are paid by the hour, or occasionally salaried. This way the employee expense is a relatively controlled figure based on the hours worked. This simplifies the stock work as the employee does not make a different rate for this service. However, in this scenario it is important that a shop manager monitor the billing charges to customers to guard against too much "free or undercharged work" as they receive the same amount of pay regardless of billings fees.

Future

Service work will always be a component of the music industry. The types of skills necessary to excel in this area have changed over the years as electronic and digital technologies have invaded many parts of the industry. As the internet and large chain stores continue to grow, service work will become an increasingly important way for brick and mortar stores to add value to the products they carry and remain competitive in the future.

The Music Products Industry

Chapter 10

Careers in the Music Products Industry

Determining a career path in the music products industry is an exciting challenge. Many people enter into the industry initially because they are musicians and want a "day gig" between musical performances. Often, they find that a steady paycheck and job stability is more attractive than life on the road. Frankly, the vast majority of people working in the music products industry not only have music backgrounds, but are still actively working musicians. In fact, working in the industry often helps the musicians become more connected and leads to a satisfying career in music.

Today, however, we find more and more young people entering the music products industry with the intention of making a career in the business of music. While formal education was once looked upon as a bonus for people entering the industry, now having a degree in "music business or music industry" is often a requirement.

For many, the end goal is to work for a major musical instrument manufacturer. However, these employers often insist that their staff have previous retail work experience. They feel it is vital to have worked with the end consumer before being employed further up the food chain. Many find that working at the retail level is the most rewarding, being closest to the actual musicians.

The Music Products Industry

There are many different paths to success in the products industry. The following guide is to help people discover the many opportunities for careers in the music products industry.

Retail Salesperson - Initially an entry level position, good salespeople can make a healthy living working the sales floor, especially in parts of the products industry where higher dollar products are sold.

Retail School Service Educational Representative - The school service business is often done outside of the traditional store. The Ed Rep's job is to establish relationships with music educators, sell or rent instruments and accessories, and provide service and support for the music programs.

Retail Manager/Owner - Managers and owners are responsible for all of the day to day operations of a retail floor. Purchasing duties, personnel management, inventory control, and facilities logistics all fall into the day to day responsibilities of an owner or manager.

Retail Sheet Music Specialist - Basically, these are salespeople who specialize in sheet music sales. Attention to detail, research abilities, and a working knowledge of music theory and history are important characteristics to be successful in this department.

Print Publisher Salesperson - Working for a specific publisher, this person sells their catalog of music to the retailer. Music theory and history knowledge are important here as well.

Print Publisher Editor - As an editor the responsibilities include discovering new composer submissions for the catalog. Editing duties include analyzing the new submissions for accuracy and clarity as well as determining proper pricing and marketing for the music.

Wholesale Sales Representative - Representing a wholesale distributor for music accessories and instruments, relationships are built between the wholesaler and the retail music store. Most often, sales are done over the phone and may cover a vast territory.

Instrument Manufacturer District Manager - This person's responsibilities include developing franchise relationships with retail music stores, marketing their products, and protecting their brand identity. Depending on the size of their territory, extensive travel is usually common. Exhibiting at trade shows, clinics, and other events is often part of promoting the brand.

Instrument Manufacturer Product Manager - The duty of the product manager is to market a sub-category of products for the manufacturer. Developing sales programs, handling warranty issues, dealing with suppliers, and creating brand identity all fall into the scope of this position.

Instrument Manufacturer Artist Relations - As part of the promotion of the brand, the A&R manager finds professional musicians to endorse their products. Artists may also be brought in to assist with design ideas for new products.

Instrument Warranty and Design - This job involves handling warranty issues for customers, investigating the cause of problems, and designing solutions to incorporate into new models. Generally, a background in service and repair is required.

Instrument Repair - Similar to the warranty duties described above, instrument repair staff work at the retail level either as retail employees or independent contractors. Service and repair is done both for consumers and for retail stock inventory.

Piano Tuner and Restoration - As yet another branch of the service industry, piano tuners regulate acoustic pianos. For some, full restoration and rebuilding of the instruments may be offered as part of their service.

Chapter 11

Our Little Industry Giant

The music products industry is one of the most overlooked industries for young music business professionals. Globally, it has a 17 billion dollar capitalization. It eclipses the entire music recording industry that gets much more of the glamour and attention. While large in scale relative to other parts of the music industry, the products side is still relatively small compared to many other industries. This dichotomy creates a nice balance. Professionals entering the industry are able to not only achieve employment but set themselves up for advancement through the industry. Whether that route is through the retail side, the manufacturing path, or some combination of the two, there are many opportunities to learn the business.

While the industry seems somewhat intimidating at first, the reality is that it is comparably small and friendly. As such, it is not unusual for a newcomer to the industry to be rubbing shoulders with the CEO of a major manufacturer in almost no time at all. The NAMM show has been such a great way to not only learn about new products and create trade relationships, but to network with fellow music professionals. It has often been said that NAMM is simply a giant family reunion where a trade show breaks out!

Professionals working in the music products industry come from all different backgrounds. Some are working professional musicians who are looking for further stability in their careers. Others were once educators who chose to change their career path. Today, however, having a collegiate education in Music Business or Music Industry is a great way to prepare for this field. NAMM's Generation Next initiative works hard at preparing the next generation to enter into the music products industry.

However one enters the industry, it can be a rewarding career that allows professionals the opportunity to change lives and enhance the future of music in our culture. Good luck!

Glossary

Accounts receivables - Assets that are owed to a company. Sales made on time payments for which cash has not yet been received.

Accumulated earned discounts - The process of earning larger discounts based on total sales to date rather than a single purchase.

Big box store - Large, mass merchandise retailers.

Brick and mortar - Retailers with a physical presence rather than just online web interface.

Buying cycles - How often a customer is ready to repurchase a similar item.

Carry the paper - Keeping the financing internal. Not selling it to an outside financier.

Classical guitar - Acoustic guitar with nylon strings and often no pickguard or truss rod. Used in classical literature and for plucking melodies.

College sampler - An instrument used on loan to a university music program, generally for an instrumental methods class or classroom use.

Conversion rate - The number of customers that change from renting to a purchasing commitment.

Cost of entry - The price a customer spends to begin using a basic product.

Curtailment - A payment made to shorten the life of a loan often used in floor planning agreements.

Digital printing press - Effectively a giant copy machine used to print music on demand for specific customers rather than inventorying large batches.

Display season - The process of displaying and renting beginning band instruments, often directly at a school location. Also known as a rental drive.

Dreadnought guitar - Acoustic guitar with steel strings and a large, traditional body. The most common style of guitar marketed.

Dry hire - The process of leasing commercial audio equipment with no further technical support.

Dealer agreement - The legal document outlining the terms of trade between a retailer and a manufacturer.

E-Commerce retailer - Selling products through a web store interface.

End column - The largest discount available to a dealer from a manufacturer.

Endorsement deals - A contract between a manufacturer and a performing artists that uses and recommends the manufacturer's product.

Extended dating - Terms of repayment offered to a dealer from a manufacturer beyond the customary 30 days.

Factoring company - A financial institution that purchases the receivables from a retailer in exchange for a discounted valuation.

Fall dating - Extended terms of repayment offered to a dealer often found in the school band and orchestra business. Repayment is not required until after the traditional fall rental season.

Floor planning - An agreement where the inventory on a retailer's showroom is financed through an outside financial institution.

Freight allowance - A discount towards shipping charges often based on the dollar amount of the purchase.

House brands - Proprietary brands that feature the name of the specific dealer instead of the manufacturers. Also known as stencil brands.

Humbucker pickup - A common type of transducer that is found on electric guitars and resists outside noise interference.

Inventory - Products that a dealer keeps in stock and are available for sale.

Just in time - Inventory that is purchased by the retailer or manufacturer and is immediately sold.

Lease pool - Inventory that is purchased by a dealer, expensed as capital goods, and then rented to customers with no equity accumulation.

Manufacturer's Suggested Retail Price (MSRP) - The standard price a manufacturer uses to both establish value and to create dealer discount structures.

Minimum Advertised Pricing (MAP) - The lowest price a dealer is allowed to show to the public in print or e-commerce. This often creates the average sale price to the public.

Master order - A large stock order placed with a manufacturer often with better discounts or extended repayment terms.

New Issue Program - A print music inventory agreement which automatically ships a print publisher's newly released music to a retailer for sale.

Paper houses - A music retailer that only carries sheet music.

Print cost - The price charged by a print publisher to a dealer for music given away at clinics or used for other promotional purposes.

Print publisher - A publisher that focuses on the reproductive copyright for music and uses a printing press to make copies for sale to dealers.

Pro Audio Combo (PAC) - The segment of the music products industry that includes guitars, amplifiers, and other related pop music products.

Proprietary brands - Product brands that are unique to a specific manufacturer or have limited distribution to its dealer network.

Publisher - A company that secures the copyright for music and monetizes those rights in various ways for the composer.

Rental and staging - A company in the business of providing pro audio equipment for live shows that do not carry their own gear.

Rental drive - The process of displaying and renting beginning band instruments, often directly at a school location. Also known as the display season.

Rental returns - Instruments that have been leased out and returned by a customer for re-rental or resale.

Rent to own - Inventory that is leased out from salable inventory with a method to accumulate rental credit towards purchase.

Sideways sales - A sale by one retailer to another non-competing authorized retailer done to rebalance inventory.

Stencil brands - Proprietary brands that feature the name of the specific dealer instead of the manufacturers. Also known as house brands.

Step-up instruments - Premium or professional grade instruments that are above a standard, student quality.

Stock orders - A large order placed with a print publisher often with better discounts or extended repayment terms.

Stocking programs - An inventory agreement between a print publisher and a dealer that provides returnable stock to the dealer on a temporary basis.

Turn cycle - The time it takes for a specific category of inventory to fully be sold at a retailer, sometimes known as sell-through.

Wet hire - The process of leasing commercial audio equipment with additional technical support personnel included.

The Music Products Industry

Carl Anderson

The Music Products Industry